Credits

Publisher: Richard Abrams
Editor-in-Chief: David Dockterman

◆————————————————◆

The Graph Club was designed by Peggy Healy Stearns, Ph.D.

Original Macintosh Version
Implementation and additional design: Shawn Cokus
Product Manager: Bruce Michael Green
Assistant Product Manager: Peter Reynolds

Updated Macintosh Version
Programming support and adaptation: Sean Nolan
Product Manager: Laurel Kayne

Windows Version
Product Manager: Jessica Adler
Software Project Leader: Jim Park
Software Engineers: Bryan Dube, Eric VanHelene
Software Technical Leader: Bruce Rosenblum
Programming Support: Eytan Bernet

Editorial
Documentation: Research/Writing/Editorial: Peggy Healy Stearns
Managing Editor: Annette Donnelly
Proofreading: Janet Reynolds
Suggested Reading List: Mary Jo Melvin

Art and Design
Program Graphics and Icons: Robert Thibeault, Robert Keough, Liz Hurley
Design & Production: Laurie Bennett, Sharon LeBoeuf-Dubois, Christine Barie
Teacher Guide Illustrations: Peter Hamilton Reynolds
Music: Gerry and Gordy Stearns

Thanks to the team at Tom Snyder Productions
Sam Ackerman, Cam Ackland, Carl W. Adams, Jessica Adler, Chris Akelian, Martha Akers, Anthony Allen, Seth Alpert, Julie Angorn, Maxim Antinori, Eytan Bernet, Loren Bouchard, Max Coniglio, Amy Conklin, Jennifer Connelly, Becky Conners, Robert Daley, Aldina Dias, Peter Elarde, Bill Eldridge, Hedrick Ellis, Peter Erwin, Carrie Finison, Maria Flanagan, Chris Georgenes, Rebecca Georgenes, Lisa Gillim, Pip Gilmour, Sharon Glick, Rishava Green, Naomi Angorn Halpern, Lisa Hamanaka, Arlene Hawkins, Lisa Heaney, Niki Hebert, Ruta Kulbis, Michelle Lauder, Annette Cate LeBlanc, Karen LeBlanc, Richard Luongo, André Lyman, Amy MacDonald-Ronayne, Kathy Manning, Lisa Marenghi, Christie McQueen, Melissa Mixer, Peter Mullin, Kim O'Neil, James Reidy, Sandy Reilly, Ivan Rhudick, John Rielly, Jenny Robinson, John Sacco, Jessica Sandel, Paul Santucci, Jennifer Schulman, Tom Snyder, Mark Usher, Steven Veverka, Kathleen Weller, Christopher Werler, Jim Woodell, and Amy Yau

Special thanks to the following educators:
Judi Adams, Ellen Baru, Diane Boehm, Karen Bryant, Gary Carnow, Barbara Chmura, Frances Curcio, Bob Densmore, Lori Deuchar Yum, Pat Dolan, Chris Dowd, Peter Flyzik, Mirium Furst, Lori Gern, Marianne Handler, Meg Henderson, Frances Malloway, Michelle Marriott, Kam Matray, Paula McGirr, Pat Messina, Karen Michalak, Marilyn Nicholson, Ted Perry, Linda Polin, Joe Proscia, Mary Vesneske, Judy Yacio

◆————————————————◆

For further information about Tom Snyder Productions or for a free catalog, call us at
1-800-342-0236

Contents

Notes from the Field

Hundreds of educators have used *The Graph Club* in their classrooms. Here's what they are saying:

"At last! Here is a truly flexible, easy-to-use, yet sophisticated 'thinking' resource for both learning and teaching. As a learning resource, it's perfect for individual and collaborative critical or creative thinking activities. As a teaching resource, it supports all the essential elements of fine instruction both in and out of the math classroom."

Kam Matray, Director, California Model Technology Schools Project, Monterey, California

"The Graph Club is OUTSTANDING! It makes graphs understandable for students of all ages. It's fun!"

Diane Boehm, Texas Computer Education Association Teacher of the Year 1992, Saint Andrew's Episcopal School, Austin, Texas

"I feel The Graph Club will revolutionize the teaching of graphing skills at the primary level. It is easy and fun to create graphs, and I was very pleased at how well my Kindergartners analyzed the changes taking place as they placed the icons for their choices in the graph. Since they all were able to participate in the creation of the graph, they felt as though the graph reflected their thoughts and feelings. I posted the graphs we made and the children remained highly interested in assessing the printouts long after the lessons were finished."

Karen Bryant, Kindergarten Teacher, Apple Early Learning Connections Demonstration Site, Yorkshire Central Schools, Yorkshire, New York

A Note from the Author

Graphs, like other kinds of pictures, tell a story at a glance. Most people would rather read a graph than a page full of numbers. And even though reading a graph takes only a fraction of the time, one generally ends up with a much better understanding of the data. In this age of information overload, when students come to our classrooms visually oriented anyway, graphs are a powerful adjunct to the written word. We can share this power with our students.

The Graph Club is designed to do just that. Its highly manipulative and interactive environment can help children make the transition from graphing with manipulatives to graphing in the abstract and help them see that the same data can be represented differently. Using *The Graph Club*, children learn to gather, sort, and classify information; they construct graphs, analyze their data, and print their graphs in multiple sizes. They learn to use graphs to solve problems and make decisions, and they talk about, write about, and share their graphs.

The Graph Club is an exciting and effective tool which can be used in any area of the curriculum, from math and science to language arts, social studies, and more. We hope you and your students find *The Graph Club* a fun and motivating environment in which to explore, play, think, and learn about the power of graphs.

Peggy Healy Stearns

What Is *The Graph Club*?

A Hands-on Graphing Tool

The Graph Club provides a motivating, manipulative environment within which you can structure your entire graphing unit. It was designed to help students in grades K–4 develop the ability to read and interpret graphs and use graphs to communicate information, answer questions, and solve problems. *The Graph Club* assists children in making the transition from graphing with manipulatives to graphing in the abstract and helps them understand the relationship between different representations of the same data — e.g., picture graph, bar graph, line graph, circle graph, and table. It is designed to **support the NCTM standards** and encourage cooperative learning, problem solving, and cross-curricular integration.

Students learn that data comes from many sources and that it is used for a variety of purposes. Students can collect information from class surveys, interviews, reading, and other research. They can use data to organize and communicate information, answer questions, make decisions, and solve problems.

A Flexible Curriculum Resource

The Graph Club is a powerful, open-ended tool which can be used to support and enhance graphing activities across the curriculum. The suggestions on pages 27–33 will give you some ideas on how best to utilize the program. See pages 34–36 for suggested graphing ideas.

Sample Graphs

A set of 35 sample graphs — 25 Explore graphs and 10 Match graphs — have been included with the software. They cover a variety of subjects and graphing skills. While it's easy to design your own graphs and activities, we've included these sample graphs as ready-to-go graphing activities for busy teachers. See pages 37–72 for full-page printouts of the graphs.

Many Printing Options

All graphs can be printed in three sizes — standard, big book, or poster. A title box and a text box in the print option encourage students to write about their graphs. Titles and descriptions can be printed with the graphs and saved with the graph file.

Range of Applications

You'll discover that although *The Graph Club* was designed for grades K–4, the program has exciting potential at the upper elementary and middle school levels. Circle graphs, for instance, can be labeled with whole numbers, fractions, or percents; open two views of the same circle graph, label each differently (e.g., one with numbers and the other with fractions or percents) and you have a powerful interactive environment for exploring the relationship between these numerical forms. This ability to view the same data in a variety of ways provides countless opportunities for sophisticated critical thinking and problem solving activities.

Learning Objectives

Content Goals

Students will create and interpret the following types of graphs in both concrete and abstract form:

+ Tables
+ Picture graphs
+ Bar graphs
+ Line graphs
+ Circle graphs

Skill and Process Goals

Students will develop the following math, problem solving, communication, cooperative learning and cross-curricular skills:

+ Counting, adding, subtracting
+ Sorting and classifying
+ Comparing
+ Generating questions
+ Determining what information is needed to answer a question
+ Collecting data via surveys, interviews, research, and other means
+ Organizing data
+ Discovering patterns
+ Interpreting data
+ Using graphs to communicate information
+ Creating and interpreting abstract representations of data
+ Using graphs to solve problems
+ Using graphs to make decisions
+ Reading, writing and talking math

What You Get & What You Need

What You Get

+ *The Graph Club* software (disks or CD-ROM)

+ Teacher's Guide, including a software WalkThrough, a guide to Features & Functions, classroom suggestions, sample activities, and more.

What You Need

Computer	System	RAM	Monitor	Hard Disk	CD-ROM Drive	Optional
Macintosh LC II (68030 processor) or higher	6.0.7 or later	1 meg available	black & white or color	required for floppy disk version	required for CD-ROM version	large-screen projection device, external speakers
Macintosh Power PC						
IBM-compatible* 386/33 processor or higher	Windows 3.1 or later	4 megs	VGA or better			
* *Note:* To hear sounds you must have a Windows-compatible sound card.						

Optional Curriculum Kit

We've developed a complete, interdisciplinary graphing curriculum for use with *The Graph Club*. It is based on an original chapter book and contains 100 ready-to-use graphing activities. *The Graph Club Curriculum Kit* includes a software template disk which works with this version of *The Graph Club*, one copy of *Fizz & Martina's Not-For-Profit Pet Resort Mystery*, an Activities Guide, and 28 student books (7 sets of 4 different books which guide a myriad of cooperative learning activities). *The Graph Club Curriculum Kit* is available for both Macintosh and Windows. For more information, or to place an order, just call our Sales and Support Team at **1-800-342-0236**.

Quick Install & Easy Start

Quick Install

CD-ROM Version

Macintosh: Insert the CD-ROM and double-click the program icon.

Windows 3.1: Insert the CD-ROM. From the **Program Manager,** choose **Run** from the **File** menu. Type **D:SETUP** (where D is your CD-ROM drive), and click **OK.** Follow the on-screen instructions.

Program Icon

Windows 95/98: Insert the CD-ROM, double-click the CD-ROM icon, then double-click the program icon to start the program.

Disk Version

The Graph Club installer

Macintosh: Insert Install disk 1 and double-click the installer icon. Follow the on-screen instructions.

Windows: Insert Install disk 1 into drive **A.**
- For Windows 3.1: go to the **Program Manager** and choose **Run** from the **File** menu. Type **A:SETUP** and click **OK.** Follow the on-screen instructions.

- For Windows 95/98: go to the **Start** menu and choose **Run.** Type **A:SETUP** and click **OK.** Follow the on-screen instructions.

Easy Start

The WalkThrough on page 12 provides a simple tour that introduces you to the software. If you prefer to explore on your own, here is an abbreviated road map to help you navigate solo.

Four Modes

The Graph Club has four modes: Explore, Match, Create, and Guess.

Main Menu (Macintosh)

Explore mode provides two side-by-side graphs and lets you and your students do the rest. Change one graph and the other changes simultaneously. Open additional graphs and see your data up to five different ways: picture, bar, circle, line, table.

Match mode sets up one graph with randomly generated data, and one blank graph. Students are challenged to fill in the blank graph to match the existing one.

Create mode generates a blank table with the data set to zero. Enter your numeric data, then choose **Make Another Graph** from the **Graph** menu and view your data different ways.

Guess mode generates a graph and challenges your students to hypothesize about what the data might represent.

Basic Features & Functions

Below is an example of a graph created in Explore mode. Highlighted are basic operations, such as adding data and changing the view of your data. Be sure to explore the many options available through the menu items. For an explanation of any menu item, please refer to Features & Functions on page 19.

Drag icons from these bins into the windows to create graphs. Once your graph is started, you can click graph elements (such as the top of a bar) and drag them to add or delete data quickly.

Click here to change the y-axis label.

Click here to change scale.

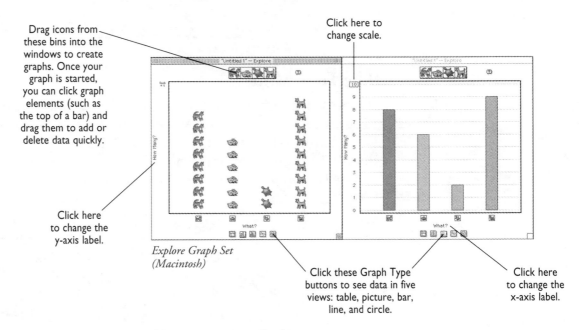

Explore Graph Set (Macintosh)

Click these Graph Type buttons to see data in five views: table, picture, bar, line, and circle.

Click here to change the x-axis label.

Note: If you have the Bilingual version of *The Graph Club*, you can toggle back and forth between English and Spanish by choosing English or Español from the Special menu. For more information, see page 26.

WalkThrough

Install the Software

See page 10 for instructions on installing the software.

Introduction

Click **Play Introduction** when the title screen appears, then click the arrows in the lower right corner to scroll through the introduction.

Title Screen (Macintosh)

The Four Modes

At the **Main** menu, you will see *The Graph Club*'s four program modes: **Explore, Match, Create**, and **Guess**. Click **Explore** to select it, then click **OK**. For a more detailed explanation of the modes, please refer to Using *The Graph Club*'s Four Modes on page 27.

Main Menu (Macintosh)

Making a Graph in Explore Mode

Entering data

3. Move your cursor to the orange cat at the top of the graph on the left. Hold the mouse button down and drag a cat into the area above the cat icon at the bottom of the graph.

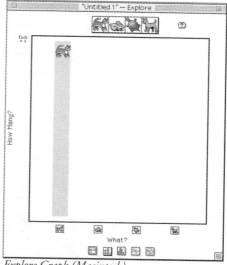

Explore Graph (Macintosh)

When the cat is in the correct area, a highlighted column will appear, and you will hear "bing." Release the mouse at this time, and you will have graphed one cat! Notice that on the bar graph to the right you also have one cat.

4. Click the **bar graph** to select it, then click the top of the orange bar, hold the mouse down, and drag the bar up or down to change data.

5. Enter data for all four animals until you have a graph to your liking.

Cool Feature: Copy graphs from *The Graph Club* and paste them into any paint or draw program! For directions, see page 21.

Having Some Fun

Graph 5 kinds

6. Now go to the **Graph** menu and choose **Graph 5 Kinds**. Notice that there are now five "icon bins" above your graph, and there is a bird in the fifth bin for you to graph.

Choose symbols

7. Go back to the **Graph** menu and choose **Choose Symbols**... The following screen will appear. (*Note:* The picture below shows a Macintosh screen. The Windows screen is slightly different.)

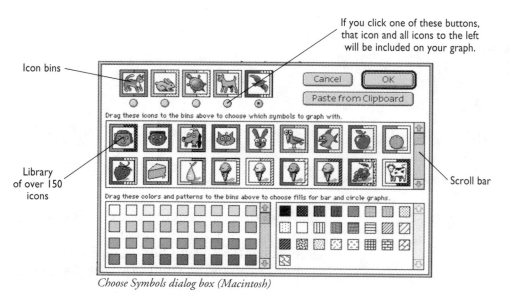

Choose Symbols dialog box (Macintosh)

8. Scroll through the library of icons until you find a few favorites. To add an icon to your graph, simply click it and drag it up to the icon bin. Experiment with replacing all five icons in your graph.

Cool Feature: In addition to choosing icons, you can choose a range of colors and patterns for circle and bar graphs.

Extra-cool Feature: You can design your own symbols in any paint or draw program and import them into *The Graph Club.* For directions, see page 22.

9. Click **OK** to return to your graph.

Graph types

10. Make sure the picture graph is selected (click it) and move your cursor to the **Graph Type** buttons at the bottom of your graph.

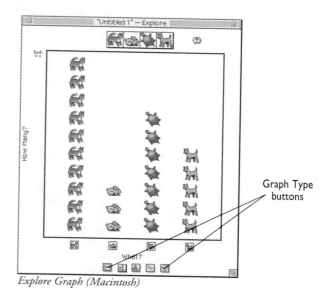

Explore Graph (Macintosh)

Notice that the picture graph button is in color. Click the circle graph button, then experiment with the other **Graph Type** buttons.

Cool Feature: Using the Make Another Graph option in the Graph menu, you can open up additional graphs, resize them to fit on the screen together, and see your data represented multiple ways. (**Note:** Your computer's resolution will determine the number of graphs that can fit on screen without overlapping.)

Scale maximum

11. Using the **Graph Type** buttons, select a circle graph and a bar graph. Next go to the **Graph** menu and choose **Choose Scale Maximum**. Click 200, then click **OK**.

Note: The scale maximum for picture graphs is 20.

Cool Feature: On your bar graph, notice the box at the top of the Y axis that says 200. You can change the scale maximum by clicking this box. This option is available for bar, picture, and line graphs.

Entering and deleting data

Now let's add some more data to your graphs — we'll try two different ways to do this.

12. Drag an icon into its corresponding segment in your circle graph. This adds one unit to your graph.

13. Now move the mouse to the edge of a segment and drag it clockwise. This allows you to add data more rapidly to your graph. Moving the mouse counterclockwise deletes data from the graph.

Note: The dragging method of changing data is available for bar, circle, and line graphs.

Cool Feature: You can label your circle graph 5 different ways. Click a number on your circle graph. Notice that you can select icons, numbers, fractions, percents, or no labels at all. (You can open this same dialog box by choosing Circle Graph Labels from the Options menu.)

Axis labels

14. Go to your bar graph and click **What?** above the **Graph Type** buttons. Enter a label for the X axis. Do the same for the Y axis by clicking **How Many?** Finally, click one of the little icons along the X axis and enter a label for the icon.

Cool Feature: With tables, you can add a title as well as axis and icon labels.

Saving

Your graphs are surely masterpieces by now, so let's save them. (All views of a given data set are saved together as one file.)

15. Choose **Save** from the **File** menu. You can also press ⌘-S (Macintosh) or Control-S (Windows).

Printing

16. To print, choose **Print Graphs** from the **File** menu. You can also press ⌘-P (Macintosh) or Control-P (Windows). Select the graph types you wish to print and they will be displayed in the Print Preview area. (You can print up to five on one page.)

Cool Feature: *The Graph Club has a special print menu designed to encourage students to write about their graphs. Enter a title and a brief description (amount of text is limited) and be sure to check the little boxes to the left of "Title" and "Description."*

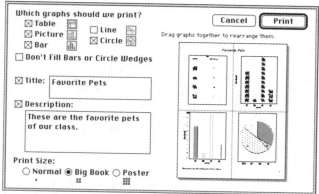

Print Graphs dialog box (Macintosh)

Match Mode

17. Choose **Close Set** from the **File** menu to close your graphs.

18. Click **Match,** then click **OK.** Your job is to create a graph on the right that matches the randomly generated graph on the left. Go to it!

19. When you have entered data in the bar graph which matches the data in the picture graph, click **Check My Match!** above the picture graph. You should see the following screen:

Click this graphic to make it disappear.

Match challenge successfully completed (Macintosh)

Note: If the program finds an incorrect match, it tells you, "Now match the others!" *The Graph Club* gives students as many tries as they need to match the graph correctly.

Cool Feature: Click **Print Certificate** for a certificate displaying the matched graphs. This is a great way to reward students' success with graphing.

Another Cool Feature: Using **Teacher Options...** in the **Special** menu, you can change the Match mode graph types and control a number of other Match mode features. For details, see Teacher Options on page 25.

Create Mode

20. Choose **Close Set** from the **File** menu.

21. Click **Create,** then click **OK**.

22. Click each zero and enter data for your table. The default scale maximum is 10, a setting you can change by choosing **Choose Scale Maximum**... from the **Graph** menu.

23. Once you have entered data for each item, go to the **Graph** menu and choose **Make Another Graph**. This allows you to see your data represented in different forms. As you open additional graphs, you may need to resize them to see them all at once.

Guess Mode

24. Close the graphs you made in Create mode. You can also press ⌘-E (Macintosh) or Control-E (Windows). Then click **Guess** and click **OK**.

This randomly generated graph gives students an opportunity to brainstorm about why someone would have made that particular graph, what it could signify, and what people could conclude from the graph.

Cool Activity: Using **New** in the **File** menu, open several Guess graphs at once (each will have the same symbols, but different data). As each graph is generated, ask students to compare the data. Challenge them to explain what underlying differences the graphs could be representing.

Cool Feature: Change the icons in the graph for a variety of critical thinking challenges.

Features & Functions

The File Menu

New: Lets you open a new graph set in any of *The Graph Club*'s four modes.

Open: Opens a previously saved graph set.

Close: Closes the selected graph view.

Close Set: Closes all the views in a graph set.

Save: Lets you save a graph set. When you save, all views of a given set are saved together.

Save As: This option lets you save a previously saved file under another name or location.

Macintosh

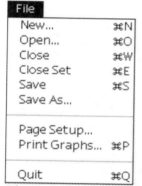

File Menu with shortcuts (Macintosh)

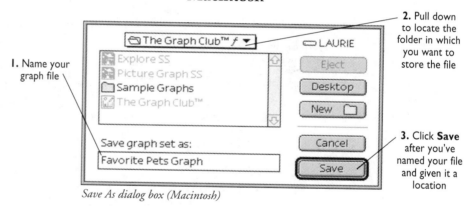

Save As dialog box (Macintosh)

1. Name your graph file

2. Pull down to locate the folder in which you want to store the file

3. Click **Save** after you've named your file and given it a location

Windows

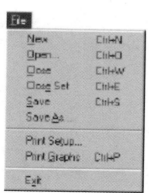

File Menu with shortcuts (Windows)

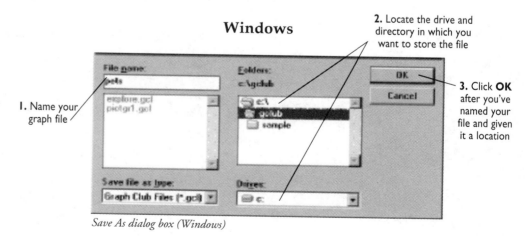

Save As dialog box (Windows)

1. Name your graph file

2. Locate the drive and directory in which you want to store the file

3. Click **OK** after you've named your file and given it a location

Page Setup (Macintosh) or **Print Setup** (Windows): Lets you set page orientation and other specifications for printing graphs.

Note: To set specifications for printing graphics, use **Print Special Setup** in the **Special** menu.

Print Graphs: *The Graph Club* print menu has a number of great features which are highlighted below. (*Note:* The picture below shows a Macintosh screen. The Windows screen is slightly different.)

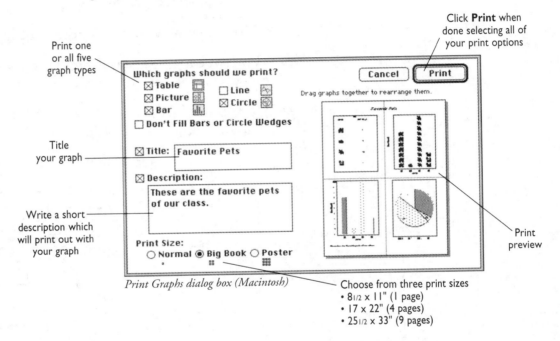

Print Graphs dialog box (Macintosh)

Cool Feature: Print in color! *The Graph Club* supports color printing (with a color ribbon). If you are using Windows, make sure to check the Color Printer box.

Quit (Macintosh) or **Exit** (Windows): Use this option to exit *The Graph Club*.

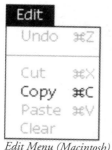

Edit Menu (Macintosh)

Edit Menu (Windows)

The Edit Menu

These are basic options found in many applications. If the Edit menu is not accessible, you can perform these actions using the appropriate shortcut keys. (***Note:*** Copy is the only function you can perform on graphs. *All* funtions can be performed on text.)

Undo: Lets you undo your last action.

Cut: Lets you remove a highlighted section in order to place it elsewhere.

Copy: Lets you duplicate a highlighted section in order to add it elsewhere.

Paste: Use this option to insert cut or copied items into your document.

Clear: Erases highlighted section.

Cool Feature: Copy graphs from *The Graph Club* and paste them into any paint or draw program! Just select a graph (by clicking on it), choose copy from the Edit menu, open a paint or draw program, and paste!

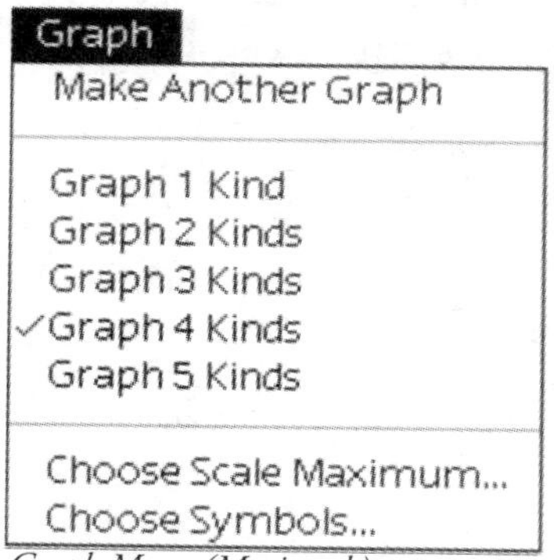

Graph
Make Another Graph

Graph 1 Kind
Graph 2 Kinds
Graph 3 Kinds
✓Graph 4 Kinds
Graph 5 Kinds

Choose Scale Maximum...
Choose Symbols...

Graph Menu (Macintosh)

The Graph Menu

Make Another Graph: Choose this option to create another view of the selected data set. The new view will appear on your desktop. You can open up to ten views of your data set. (***Note:*** If you wish to see more than two views at once, you will have to resize the windows. Your computer's resolution will determine the number of graphs that can fit on screen without overlapping.)

Graph 1 or More Kinds: These options allow you to change the number of items you are graphing. If you reduce the number of items, *The Graph Club* will eliminate symbols starting from the right. If you increase the number of items, *The Graph Club* will use the additional symbols saved with this graph.

Choose Scale Maximum: Use this option to change the scale maximum. (***Note:*** The scale maximum for picture graphs cannot exceed 20.)

Choose Symbols: Use this option to select new symbols. You can use the symbols that come with *The Graph Club* or import your own from any paint or draw program. (**Note:** The picture below shows a Macintosh screen. The Windows screen is slightly different.)

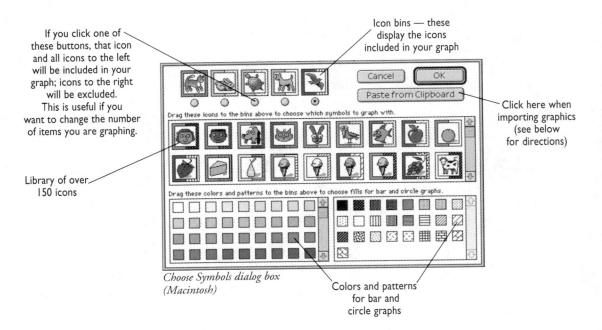

If you click one of these buttons, that icon and all icons to the left will be included in your graph; icons to the right will be excluded. This is useful if you want to change the number of items you are graphing.

Library of over 150 icons

Icon bins — these display the icons included in your graph

Click here when importing graphics (see below for directions)

Choose Symbols dialog box (Macintosh)

Colors and patterns for bar and circle graphs

To select a new icon for your graph from *The Graph Club* library of icons, simply click the icon you wish to add and drag it to the icon bin.

Cool Feature: *The Graph Club* lets you import your own graphics to use as icons. Here's how:

• Using a paint or drawing program create your own graphic.
• Copy the graphic; it will be saved in the computer's Clipboard.
• Open *The Graph Club*.
• Choose **Choose Symbols** from the **Graph** menu.
• Click **Paste from Clipboard**. The cursor will change to your icon.
• Now just click the icon bin where you wish to place your icon!

Note: Icons you import *will not* be saved in the program but *will* be saved in any new graphs you make using them.

Technical Note: Icons in *The Graph Club* library are 28 x 28 pixels. Imported icons don't have to be this size, but the closer your icons are to 28 x 28, the better they will look in the program.

Options
✓Graph Vertically
 Graph Horizontally

 Circle Graph Labels...
✓Show Bar and Line Grid
✓Show Axis Labels

Options Menu (Macintosh)

The Options Menu

Graph Vertically: This option gives your graph a vertical orientation and is the default setting whenever you create a new graph. When you choose this option, all views of the selected data set will be changed and windows will be rearranged on the screen.

Note: Some picture graphs with a scale of 20 use one icon to represent two (because of space limitations). This is noted at the top of the Y axis.

Graph Horizontally: Use this option to give graphs a horizontal orientation. All views of the selected graph will be changed and windows will automatically be rearranged on the screen. In this orientation, icon bins are on the left of the graph window and Graph Type buttons are on the right.

Circle Graph Labels: This option lets you label circle graphs five ways: with icons, numbers, fractions, percents, or no labels at all. Simply select the desired option in the dialog box and click **OK**.

Shortcut: Click any of the labels inside the circle graph to open this same dialog box.

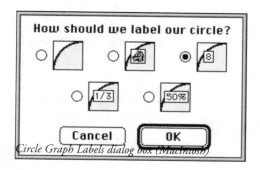

Circle Graph Labels dialog box (Macintosh)

Show Bar and Line Grid: This option lets you turn grid lines in bar and line graphs on or off. If the menu item is selected with a check mark, grid lines are on; simply reselect the option to turn the lines off.

Shortcut: Double-click any white area inside a selected graph window to turn grid lines on and off automatically.

Show Axis Labels: Select this option to show axis labels; deselect it to hide them.

Special Menu (Macintosh)

Special Menu

Edit Groups: This option allows you to add and edit classes for use with the Random Student Picker™. The Random Student Picker — a feature in many Tom Snyder Productions programs — lets you randomly select a student to enter data, answer a question, interpret a graph, or offer his or her opinion. It's a fun way to involve the entire class and keep students on their toes!

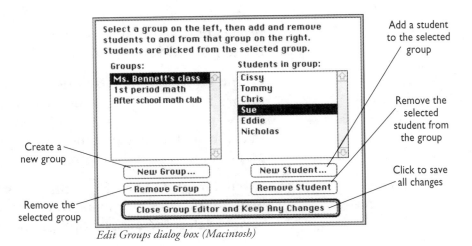

Edit Groups dialog box (Macintosh)

Pick Student: Select this option to activate the Random Student Picker.

Note: You can also choose this option by pressing ⌘-F (Macintosh) or Control-F (Windows). If you have more than one group set up, you'll need to choose **Edit Groups** and select the group you want the program to pick from before you choose **Pick Student**.

Random Student Picker (Macintosh)

To leave the Random Student Picker, just click anywhere on the graphic.

Print Special Setup: This allows you to select options for printing the special graphics that come with *The Graph Club* (available by choosing **Print Special** in the **Special** menu). Blank Match certificates, for example, should be printed landscape rather than portrait.

Print Special: We've included in *The Graph Club* a number of fun graphics including illustrations from *The Graph Club Curriculum Kit* (sold separately — see page 9 for details).

Be sure to check out *The Graph Club* logo. Print the regular version to make posters. Print the reverse version using a heat transfer ribbon in your printer (dot-matrix only) to make t-shirts for your students. You can also print blank graphing grids in three sizes for graphing activities away from the computer.

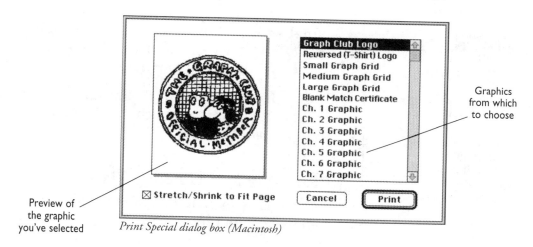

Preview of the graphic you've selected

Graphics from which to choose

Print Special dialog box (Macintosh)

Teacher Options: Teacher Options lets you customize and tailor preferences to meet the needs of your students. This option is always grayed (to restrict access). To select **Teacher Options**:

• **Macintosh:** Hold down the **Command** and **Option** keys and (without letting go) open the **Special** menu and choose **Teacher Options.**

• **Windows:** Hold down the **Shift** and **Control** keys and (without letting go) open the **Special** menu and choose **Teacher Options**.

Note: If you open the **Special** menu before pressing **Shift** and **Control**, **Teacher Options** will remain grayed.

The **Teacher Options** dialog box appears below. A Macintosh screen is shown. The Windows screen is slightly different.

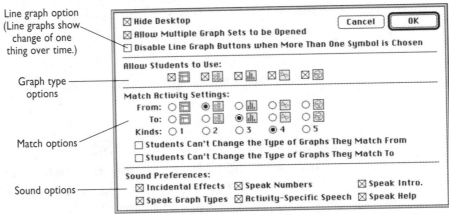

Line graph option
(Line graphs show change of one thing over time.)

Graph type options

Match options

Sound options

Teacher Options dialog box (Macintosh)

Special

Edit Groups...
Pick Student   ⌘F

Print Special Setup...
Print Special...

Teacher Options...
✓English
 Español

*Special Menu
(Macintosh Bilingual)*

English/Español: If you have the bilingual version of *The Graph Club*, you can toggle back and forth between English and Spanish using these two menu items.

Note: To read and hear the introduction in Spanish you must first enter the program, choose **Español**, then exit and restart *The Graph Club*.

Entering and Deleting Data

Below is an explanation of how to enter and delete data for all five graph types.

	Enter	Delete
Bar:	Drag icons Drag top of bar up	Drag top of bar down
Circle:	Drag icons Drag wedges clockwise	Drag wedges counter-clockwise
Line:	Drag data points up Drag icons to desired data points	Drag data points down
Picture:	Drag icons	Click icons in graph
Table:	Click number and type a new one Drag icons	Click number and type a new one

Using *The Graph Club*'s Four Modes

The following suggestions can help you make the most of *The Graph Club*'s four modes: Explore, Match, Create, and Guess. Each section below includes a brief explanation of the mode and some suggestions for using that mode.

Explore Mode

Explore mode generates a pair of graphs which let you explore graphing in an open-ended environment. Explore mode also lets you explore *The Graph Club*'s many easy-to-use features and functions. For instance, as you change one graph, the other graph changes simultaneously, allowing you to view the same data side by side in two different formats. (For details, please refer to the WalkThrough and Features & Functions.)

1. Start with a large group activity such as a class survey to familiarize students with the software.

2. Display two (or more) different representations of the same data. For example, show a table or a picture graph in the left window and a bar or circle graph in the right window.

3. Watch as the graphs take shape. Encourage students to notice how a change in one graph is reflected in other views of the same data.

4. Provide hands-on experience. Have fun changing the icons, the number of items in your graph, the scale maximum, the graph type, and the graph's orientation. Encouraging students to drag symbols and manipulate the graphs will help them make the transition from concrete to abstract representations of data. This tactile experience also supports a more sensory-oriented learning style.

5. Pump up the volume. When practical, be sure the volume is loud enough so students can hear items counted as they add to and subtract from their graphs.

6. Use the Graph Type buttons to display different views of the same data. Ask students which display is easiest for them to understand. Which do they think best represents the data? Ask students to explain their answers.

7. Discuss the graphs. Ask students questions such as:

What kind of graph is this?

What is this graph about?

What is a good title for this graph?

How many (of each kind) are there?

Of which kind is there the most? The least?

How many more (of one kind) are there than (another kind)?

Is this graph a good way to display the data?

How could you use this information?

What questions would you like to ask about this graph?

How would you like to change this graph?

Encourage students to come up with their own answers by having them write, draw, or otherwise record their response before eliciting spoken answers. When there are a limited number of possible answers, ask for a hand count to see how many students picked each answer. Ask students to give reasons for their answers.

8. Encourage students to pose questions.

9. Encourage student-initiated data collection activities. Have students conduct their own interviews, surveys, and investigations and use *The Graph Club* to display the data.

10. Graph data from other sources. Ask students to find data from another source and use *The Graph Club* to display it. Let them manipulate the data, play "what if" games, and experiment with different representations of the same data.

11. Use the saved graphs which are included with the software. These graphs — 25 Explore graphs and 10 Match graphs — are ready to use and cover a range of topics and graphing skills. Simply choose **Open** from the **File** menu and select the graph you wish to use. (See pages 37–72 for full-page printouts of these graphs.)

12. Allow students to print their graphs whenever possible. Encourage them to include a title and write a story or description in the print dialog box before printing, or write one by hand after printing.

13. Have students share and discuss their graphs.

14. Pose challenges. For example:

- Display a line graph and a bar graph. Ask students what they could do to the line graph to make all the bars in the bar graph the same height. Let them manipulate the line graph to check their predictions.

- Have students display a bar graph and a circle graph. Ask questions such as:

If you make all the bars the same height, how will the circle graph look?

If you remove one bar completely, how will the circle graph look?

After students hypothesize, let them manipulate the bar graph and see if they are right. Ask students to continue this game by asking their own questions.

- If students are sophisticated enough, introduce a discussion of fractions. Display a bar graph on the left and a circle graph on the right. Start with two bars of equal size and ask students what each part of the circle is called. Then have them change the wedge labels to fractions to see if they were right. (See Circle Graph Labels on page 23.) Ask students to predict what each wedge will be called if you add another bar of equal size.

- Display two circle graphs and label each differently — e.g., one with whole numbers and one with fractions, or one with fractions and one with percents. Compare fractions and percents. Ask students to predict how a change in one will affect the other.

15. Be alert for graphing opportunities that emerge naturally from your classroom experience. These activities will be the most meaningful and will best support your curriculum.

Match Mode

Match mode generates a random graph and challenges students to create a different type of graph which represents the same data. Match mode gives students hands-on experience reading graphs and lets them see the transformation of data from one form to another.

1. Start with an easy challenge. The program is preset to display a picture graph on the left and a bar graph on the right. Even if your students are more advanced, starting at this level will help them become familiar with the game and experience success.

2. Create easier challenges by reducing the number of items being graphed and/or using the same type of graph in each view. (See Teacher Options on page 25.)

3. Create more difficult challenges by increasing the number of items being graphed and/or using a more difficult graph type — e.g., circle.

4. Use **Choose Symbols** under the **Graph** menu (see page 22) to select interesting and relevant symbols.

5. Encourage cooperation. Have students solve Match challenges together.

6. Encourage competition. Have students take turns solving Match challenges and keep score.

7. Have students design Match challenges, save them, and then challenge their classmates.

8. Whenever possible, allow students to print the "I Matched It" certificate after completing a challenging match. Or have them print one of their random graphs and then write a story or description.

Create Mode

Create mode automatically brings up a table with each data value set to zero. This presents an opportunity for students to collect a set of data, enter it into a table in numeric form, then see those numbers transformed as they switch from a table to any of the four other graph types.

1. Have students collect data from a class survey, independent investigations, or any other source. Be sure students have their data ready, preferably recorded in list or table form, before they go to the computer.

2. Enter the data into a table, which is automatically created when you use the Create mode.

3. When students have entered their data, have them go to the **Graph** menu and choose **Make Another Graph**. Have them use the Graph Type buttons at the bottom of the picture graph to view the data in different graph forms.

4. Ask students what types of graphs are most appropriate for displaying their data. Ask them to explain their choices.

5. Encourage students to give their table a title and write or dictate a description or story about their graph in the print dialog box before printing.

6. Encourage older students to use word labels. They can do this by clicking picture labels and then entering their text.

7. Ask students to use graphs to communicate a point of view or persuade their audience.

8. Have students print graphs, color them, and share them with classmates, friends, or family. Print standard size, big book size, or poster size. Refer to Printing Ideas on page 79 for more printing ideas.

9. Be alert to graphing opportunities that emerge naturally from your classroom experiences. Encourage students to suggest graphing ideas of their own

Guess Mode

The Guess mode is designed to encourage critical thinking skills and help students understand that there are often many good answers to a question. This brainstorming activity also develops an awareness of the many different types of data that can be represented in graph form. Guess mode randomly generates graphs and challenges students to hypothesize about what the data might represent. (The data is generated randomly; you can change the icons to graph any information you choose.) Students analyze data, practice their graph-reading skills, and learn that there are often many interpretations of the same information.

For example, you could choose food icons from *The Graph Club*'s library of icons, and the program would display a graph like this one . . .

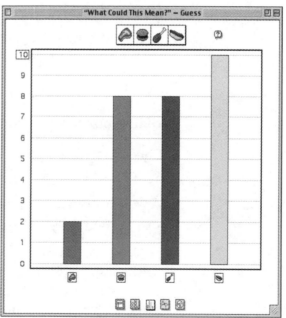

Guess Graph (Macintosh)

. . . which could be interpreted as:
Peggy: *How much a family eats in a week.*
Bruce: *The food we would have at a family picnic.*
Annette: *My third grade class's favorite meats.*
Peter: *The type of food commercials I saw on TV this week.*

1. Introduce a critical thinking activity any time you have a few unscheduled minutes. Use a large-screen monitor or projection device if available.

2. Encourage students to brainstorm as many interpretations as possible. Accept zany, imaginary interpretations as well as more mundane suggestions. Ask students to explain their answers. Then ask them to decide which interpretations are most probable.

3. Once students have suggested several interpretations for the first graph view, use the Graph Type buttons to display the data differently. Ask students which interpretations still seem plausible.

4. Type a collective description or story about your graph in the Print dialog box. The description will be saved and printed with the graph.

5. Print graphs with a story or description dictated by the class. Or print a variety of graphs without descriptions, make copies, and distribute them. Have individual students or teams brainstorm and write a logical or zany description or story about their graph. Make sure they are able to give reasons for their interpretation.

Graphing Ideas

After a few exciting adventures with *The Graph Club*, your students will begin to notice graphs in magazines, newspapers, books, television, and other media. They'll be inspired to create their own graphs and are likely to suggest all kinds of interesting topics for surveys, interviews, and investigations. Ideas that emerge naturally from the classroom experience will be the most meaningful and will best support the curriculum, so look for these opportunities and encourage students to do so.

To help you get started, we've included several dozen graphing ideas. Not all topics are appropriate for every population, so be sure to consider your student group. Select topics that are age appropriate and insure a high interest level and then enlist your students' help in identifying appropriate categories. Plan activities that actively engage your students in collecting and organizing data, creating and interpreting graphs.

Some of the following topics are ideal for picture and bar graphs, others work best as line graphs, and some suggest the use of circle graphs. Suggested graph types are noted at the top of each list. (In some cases, additional graph types might also be appropriate.) When selecting a topic, consider the type of graph students will be constructing.

Favorite Things (Table, Picture, Bar, Circle)

Beverage (*milk, juice, pop, etc.*)
Book, type of book
Candy, snack, dessert
Cereal
Color
Color for jacket, sweater, hat, etc.
Cookie
Day of the week
Dinosaur
Fast food restaurant
Fruit
Holiday
Ice cream flavor
Monster

Favorite Things (Cont.)

Movie
Pet
Planet to visit
Season
Shoes, sneakers, boots
Song
Sport to watch
Sport/game to play
Storybook character
Stuffed animal
Television show
Type of toy
Vacation spot
Vegetable
Way to spend your leisure time
Wild animal, zoo animal

How many? (Table, Picture, Bar, Circle)

Animals of specific varieties at the zoo (*lion, monkeys, giraffes, etc.*)
Birds (*robins, bluebirds, cardinals, etc.*)
Books read
Boys/girls in class, family, club, etc.
Children come to school by bus/car/bike/walk
Children have ancestors from Europe, Asia, Africa, Latin America, etc.
Children have blue/brown/black/green eyes
Children have brown/blond/red/black hair
Children have relatives in other countries
Children in your family
Children were born here/born elsewhere (*other town, state, country*)
Children's birthdays each season
Cost of different food items
Cost of different toys
Days for different seedlings to sprout
Doors in your house
Games won/lost
Goals, hits, runs, baskets
Legs different animals have
Legs different insects have

How many? (Cont.)

Sunny/rainy/cloudy/snowy days this week/month
Teeth children have lost
Television shows watched per day
Televisions/radios/telephones in household
Trash bags filled each week (*in classroom or at home*)
Trees of various kinds (*oak, pine, maple, palm, etc.*)

Measurements (Table, Bar)

Blocks/miles to school, park, shopping area
Children's height
Children's weight
Height of different seedlings/plants
Height of dolls, teddy bears, toy characters
Height/length of different animals
Hours to drive/fly to other cities
How far a frog can jump
How far students can jump
How far students can throw a ball/beanbag
How high students can climb a rope
Inches of rain/snow
Minutes to walk to cafeteria/main office/library, etc.

Dividing things up (Table, Picture, Bar, Circle)

How children spend their allowance
How children spend their waking hours
How money for a party, field trip, etc. is spent
How students share a cake, pie, cookies, pizza, apple, peanuts, etc.
Types of trash collected around classroom, school,
    community that can be recycled
Where allowance or club money comes from

How things change over time (Table, Picture, Bar, Line)

Children's height over several months
Children's foot size over several months
Height/weight/length of animals over time
Length of shadows throughout the day
Number of children who drink juice for breakfast each day
    for several days
Number of children who drink milk for lunch each day
    for several days
Plant's height over several weeks
Rainfall for several consecutive months
Temperature (high/low/average) over several days,
    weeks, or months

Sample Graphs & Activities

This section gives you a *preview* of the graphs you'll find in the Sample Graphs folder. These sample graphs are ready-to-use graphing activities you can do with your whole class. The following pages provide some fun questions you can use with the sample graphs.

There are two ways to access the sample graph files:

1. If you're running *The Graph Club*, choose **Open** from the **File** menu and navigate to the Sample Graphs folder.
2. If you're not running *The Graph Club*, simply double-click a sample graph. This will open both the sample graph and *The Graph Club*.

Important Note: Be **sure** to make a backup copy of the Sample Graphs folder on a floppy disk. Keep this disk in a safe place!

Fun Tip: *Change the graph types for additional challenges!*

Sample Graphs

Graph 1: Crazy Flavors

Brainstorm some wacky ice cream flavors, then vote for your favorites and graph the data. *If the local ice cream parlor were trying to decide on a new flavor, which one would your class suggest? Use your graph to answer the question!*

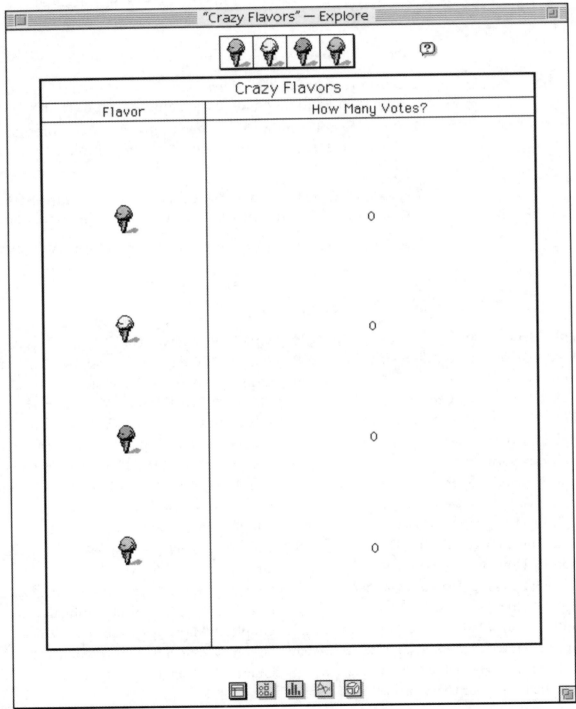

Sample Graph 1 (Macintosh)

Graph 2: Favorite Breakfast Food

Have students vote for their favorite breakfast foods and graph the data.
If your class were having a special breakfast one morning at school, which three foods would you want on the menu? Use your graph to answer the question!

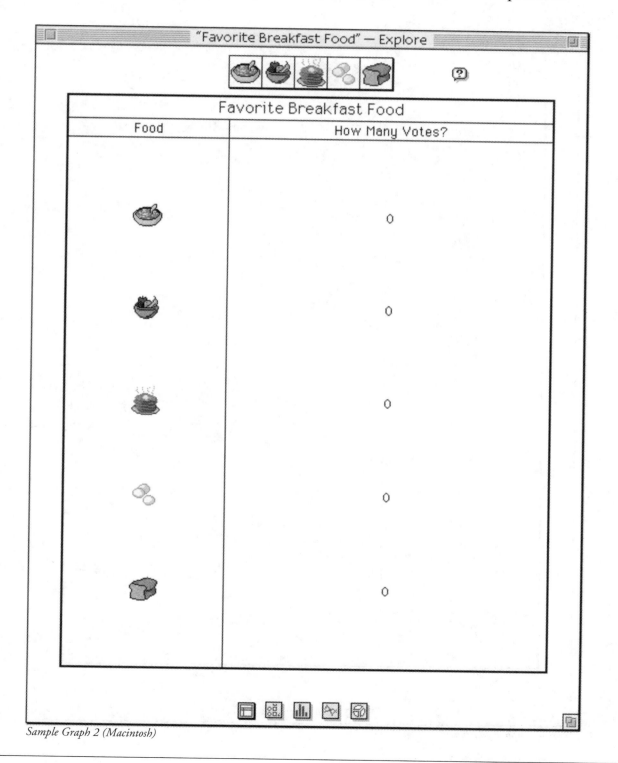

Sample Graph 2 (Macintosh)

Graph 3: Favorite Colors

Vote for your favorite colors and graph the data. *If you were going to redecorate your classroom, how could this graph help you?*

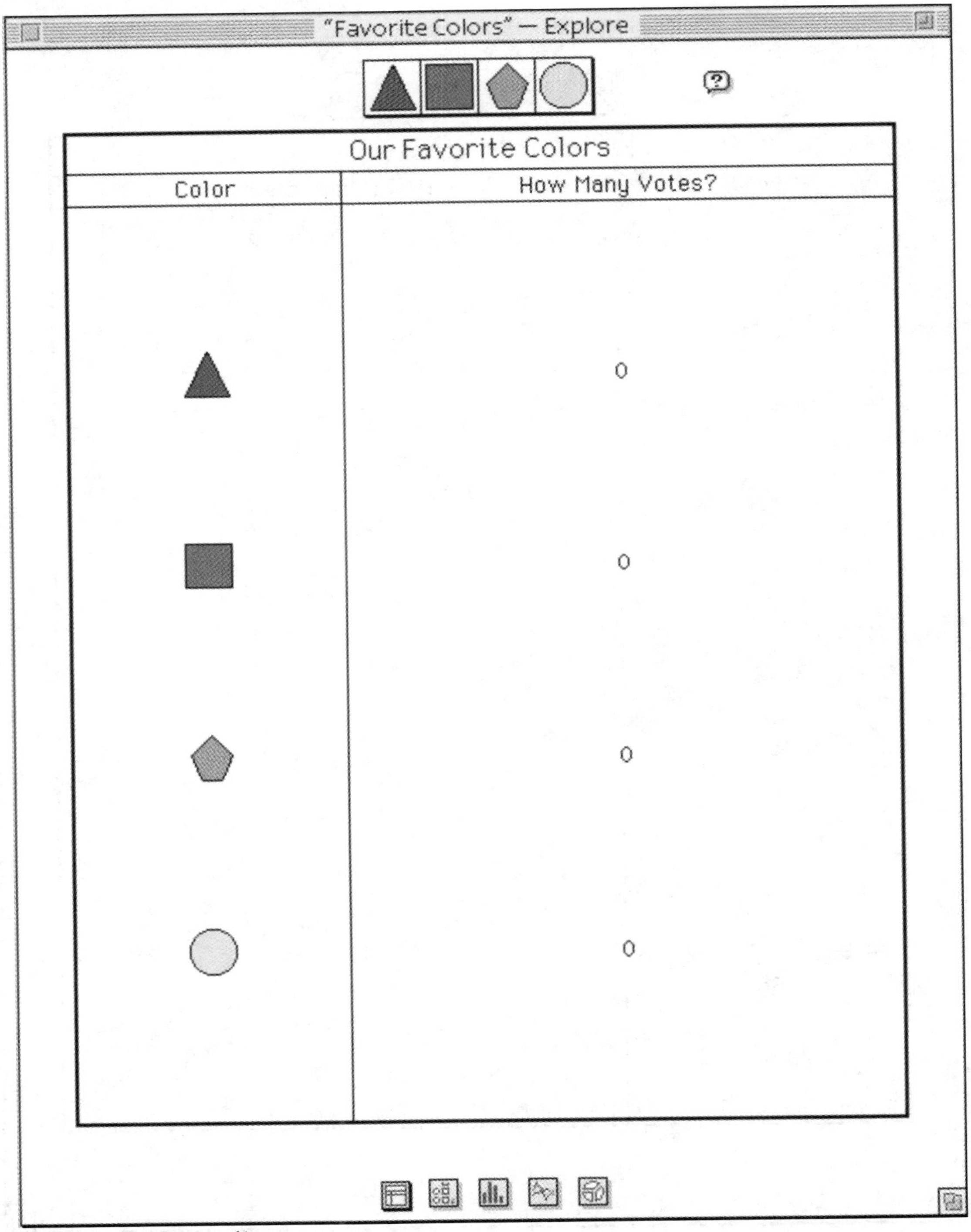

Our Favorite Colors	
Color	How Many Votes?
▲	0
■	0
⬠	0
●	0

Sample Graph 3 (Macintosh)

Graph 4: Favorite Ice Cream

Pick four popular ice cream flavors, then graph your favorites. *If your class could open an ice cream stand in the classroom with only three flavors available, which three would you pick?* Use your graph to answer the question!

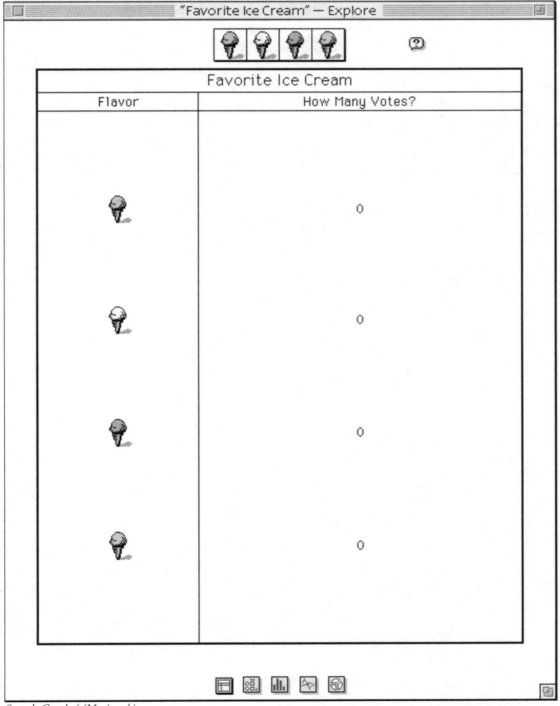

Sample Graph 4 (Macintosh)

Graph 5: Favorite Pets

Graph "favorite pet" data for your class. *If your class could adopt a pet, what animal would it be? If the local animal shelter didn't have any of that animal, what would your class's second choice be?* Use your graph to answer the questions!

Sample Graph 5 (Macintosh)

Graph 6: Favorite Season

What season do your students enjoy the most? *If your class could go on an outdoor adventure during any season, when would you go?* Use your graph to answer the question!

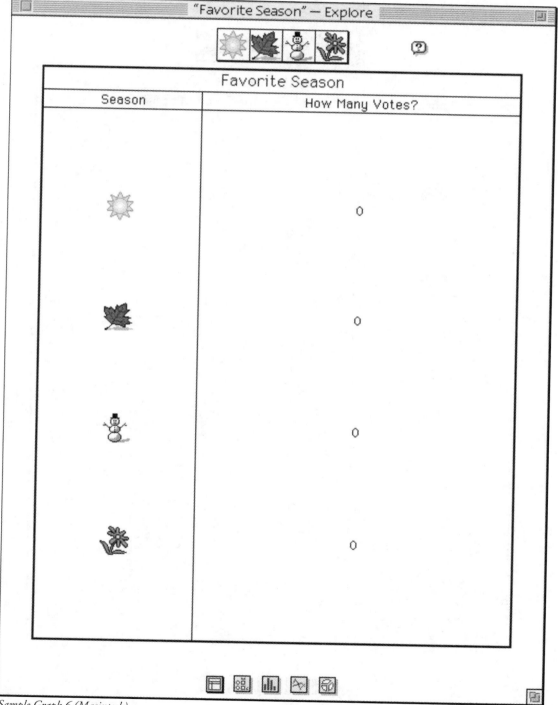

Sample Graph 6 (Macintosh)

Graph 7: Favorite Snacks

Graph your preferences for snack food. *If your class were going to have a party, and the grocery store were out of your first two choices, what food would be next on your shopping list? Use your graph to answer the question!*

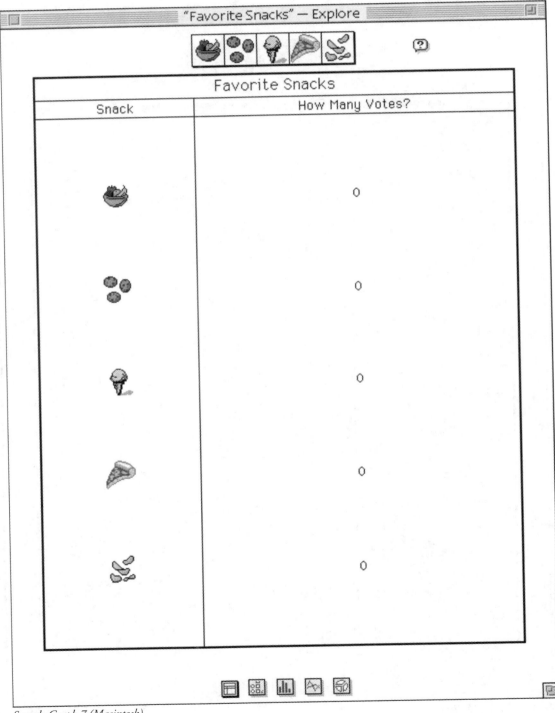

Sample Graph 7 (Macintosh)

Graph 8: Favorite Sports

Vote on your favorite sports and graph the data. *What equipment would you recommend that the principal buy for your class to use at recess?* Use your graph to answer the question!

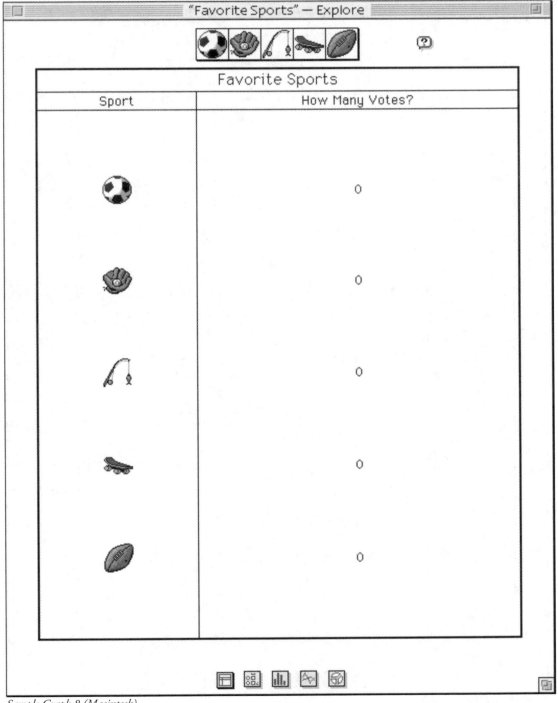

Sample Graph 8 (Macintosh)

Graph 9: Favorite Weather

What weather does your class enjoy most? *If the meteorologist in your town could **create** the weather for five days — from your 1st choice to your last — what would the weather report be for the next five days?* Use your graph to answer the question!

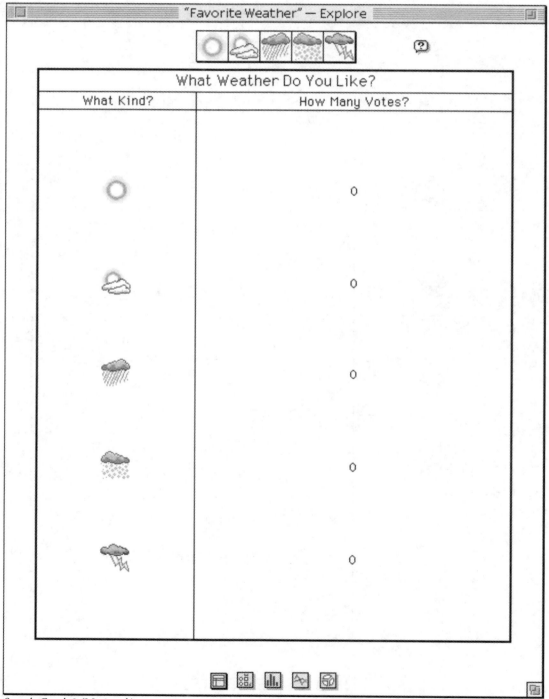

Sample Graph 9 (Macintosh)

Graph 10: Hours of TV

How many hours of TV does your class watch after school each weekday? *On what day of the week would your class have the most free time after school for a special field trip?* Use your graph to answer the question! Option: Have students graph their hours individually and compare graphs.

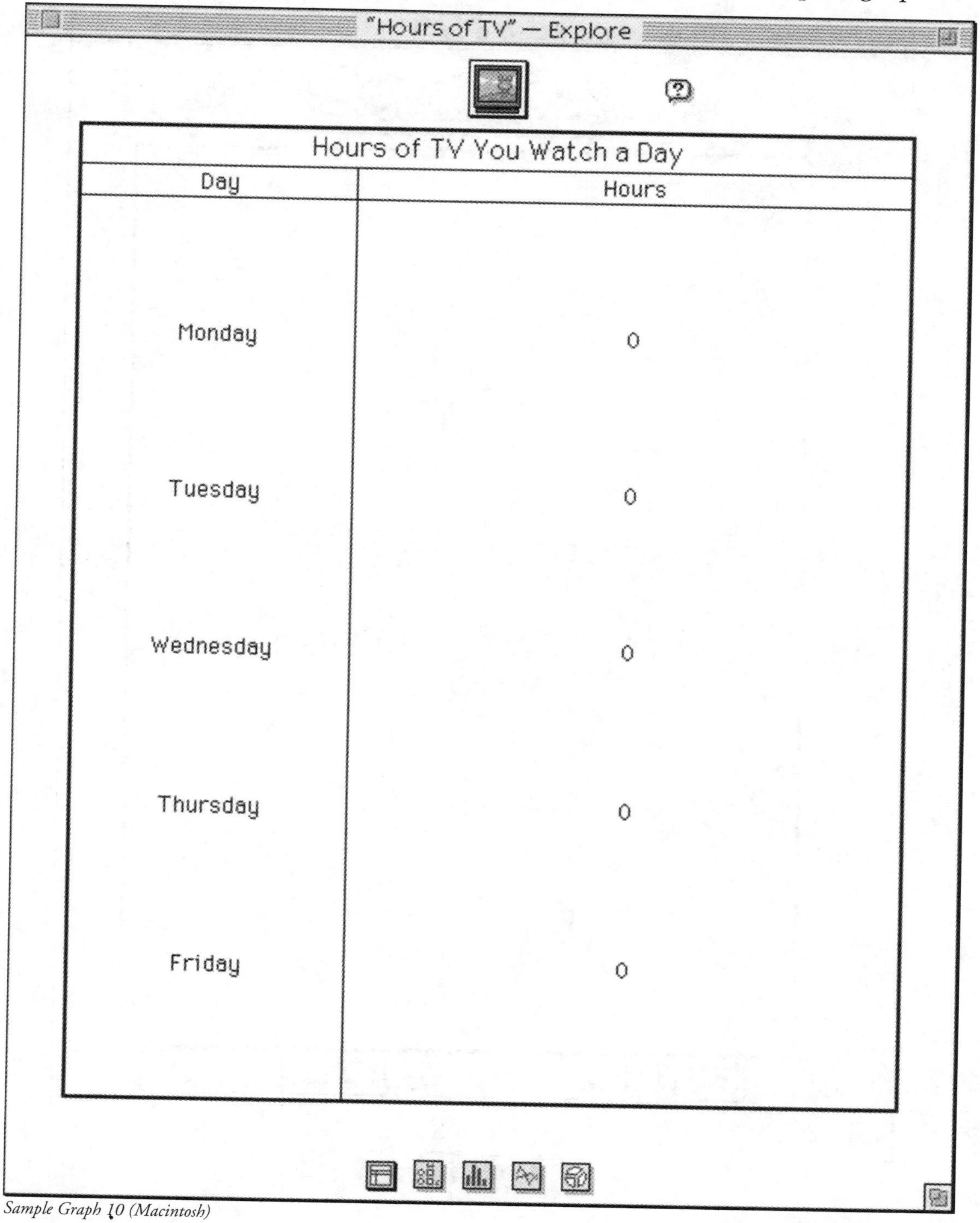

```
┌─────────────────────────────────────────────────────┐
│▪      "Hours of TV" — Explore                      ▪│
├─────────────────────────────────────────────────────┤
│                                                     │
│               ┌───┐              ?                  │
│               └───┘                                 │
│   ┌─────────────────────────────────────────────┐   │
│   │           Hours of TV You Watch a Day       │   │
│   ├──────────────────┬──────────────────────────┤   │
│   │       Day        │           Hours          │   │
│   ├──────────────────┼──────────────────────────┤   │
│   │                  │                          │   │
│   │     Monday       │            0             │   │
│   │                  │                          │   │
│   │     Tuesday      │            0             │   │
│   │                  │                          │   │
│   │    Wednesday     │            0             │   │
│   │                  │                          │   │
│   │    Thursday      │            0             │   │
│   │                  │                          │   │
│   │     Friday       │            0             │   │
│   │                  │                          │   │
│   └──────────────────┴──────────────────────────┘   │
│                                                     │
│         ▦  ▦  ▥  ▨  ▦                              │
└─────────────────────────────────────────────────────┘
```

Sample Graph 10 (Macintosh)

Graph 11: Hours You Read a Day

How many hours a day does your class read (both in and out of school)?
On what day would your class be most likely to win the Bookworm of the Day award?
Use your graph to answer the question! Option: Have students graph their
hours individually and compare graphs.

Sample Graph 11 (Macintosh)

Graph 12: How Big Are Your Feet?

Have students work in teams of five and measure their feet. As a class, graph each team's data, creating as many graphs as necessary. (Print each one as you create it, then make the next one.) *If aliens came down from space and wanted to study kids with the biggest feet and the smallest feet, who would **not** get taken away to the aliens' laboratory? Use your graphs to answer the question!*

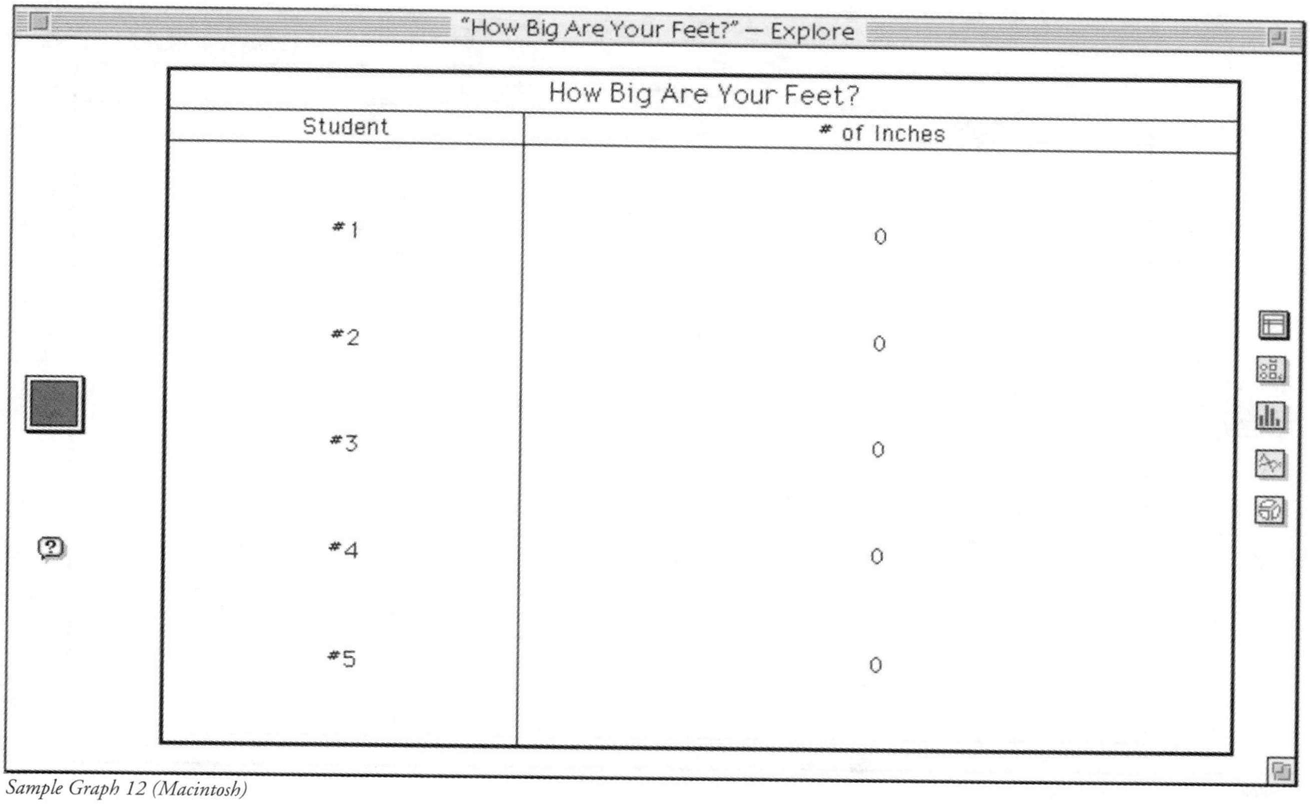

Student	# of Inches
#1	0
#2	0
#3	0
#4	0
#5	0

How Big Are Your Feet? — Explore

How Big Are Your Feet?

Sample Graph 12 (Macintosh)

Graph 13: How Big Are Your Hands?

Have students work in teams of five and measure their hands. As a class, graph each team's data, creating as many graphs as necessary. (Print each one as you create it, then make the next one.) *If you were all locked in a dungeon and the key was just a few inches away through a narrow opening, which student would have the best chance of reaching through the opening and getting the key?* Use your graphs to answer the question!

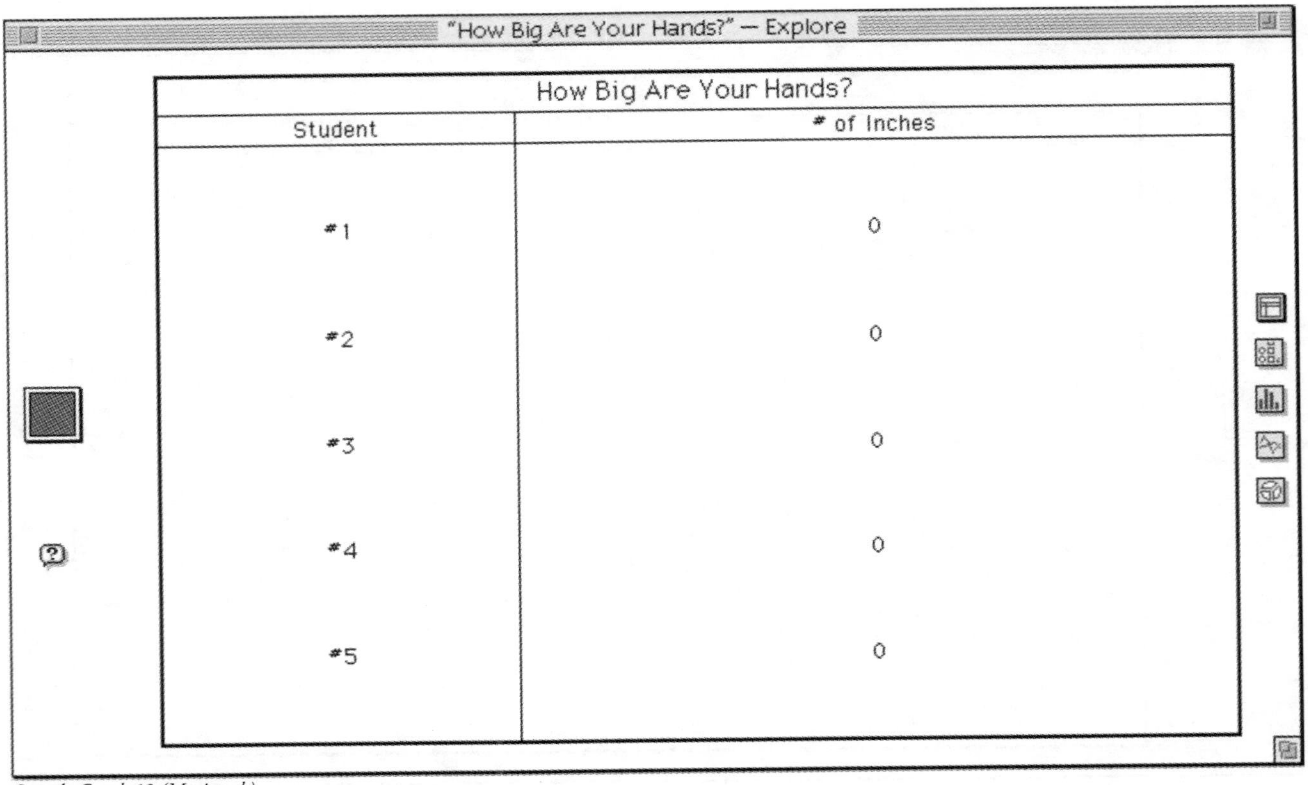

Student	# of Inches
#1	0
#2	0
#3	0
#4	0
#5	0

"How Big Are Your Hands?" — Explore
How Big Are Your Hands?

Sample Graph 13 (Macintosh)

Graph 14: How Far to School?

Figure out how far you travel to school and graph the data. *If you decided to buy a minivan and hire a chauffeur to pick up the kids who live more than two miles from school, how many seats would the van need to have?* Use your graph to answer the question!

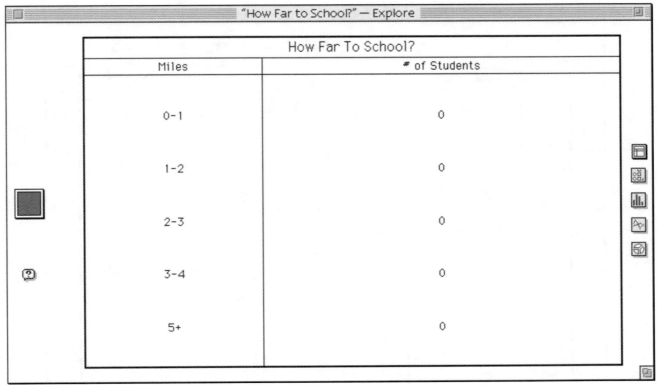

Sample Graph 14 (Macintosh)

Graph 15: How Many Would You Like?

You're having a pizza party and need to figure out how many pizzas to order. *If the pizza parlor ran out of sauce part way through your order, and kids who requested four slices had to settle for three, how many kids would have to give up a slice?* Use your graph to answer the question!

"How Many Would You Like?" — Explore

How Many Would You Like?	
# of Slices	Number of Votes
0	0
1	0
2	0
3	0
4	0

Sample Graph 15 (Macintosh)

Graph 16: How Much Rain?

Measure your rainfall for five weeks and graph the data. (If you don't get much rain, you may want to make up some data.) *During which week did the birds in your community have the most water in their bird baths? Use your graph to answer the question!*

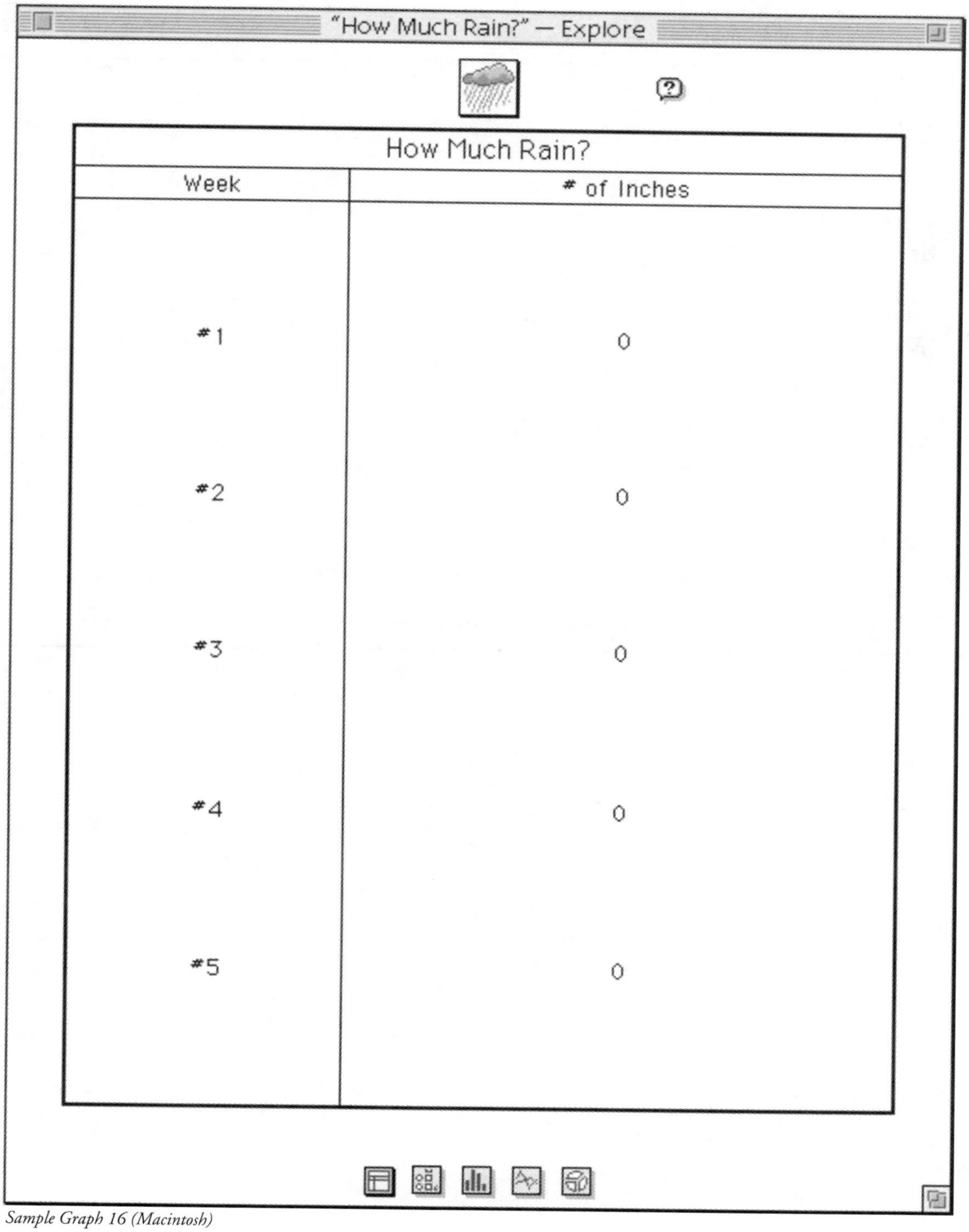

"How Much Rain?" — Explore

How Much Rain?

Week	# of Inches
#1	0
#2	0
#3	0
#4	0
#5	0

Sample Graph 16 (Macintosh)

Graph 17: How We Get to School

Survey how you get to school and graph the data. *If all motors were mysteriously shut down tomorrow, how many students would have to find another way to get to school?* Use your graph to answer the question!

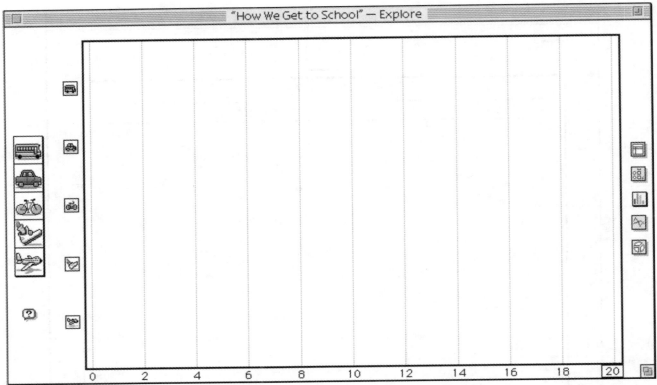

Sample Graph 17 (Macintosh)

Graph 18: Milk Your Class Drinks

Keep track of how much milk your class drinks in a week and graph the data. *If you made ice cream with your milk one day instead of drinking it, on which day would you have made the most ice cream?* Use your graph to answer the question!

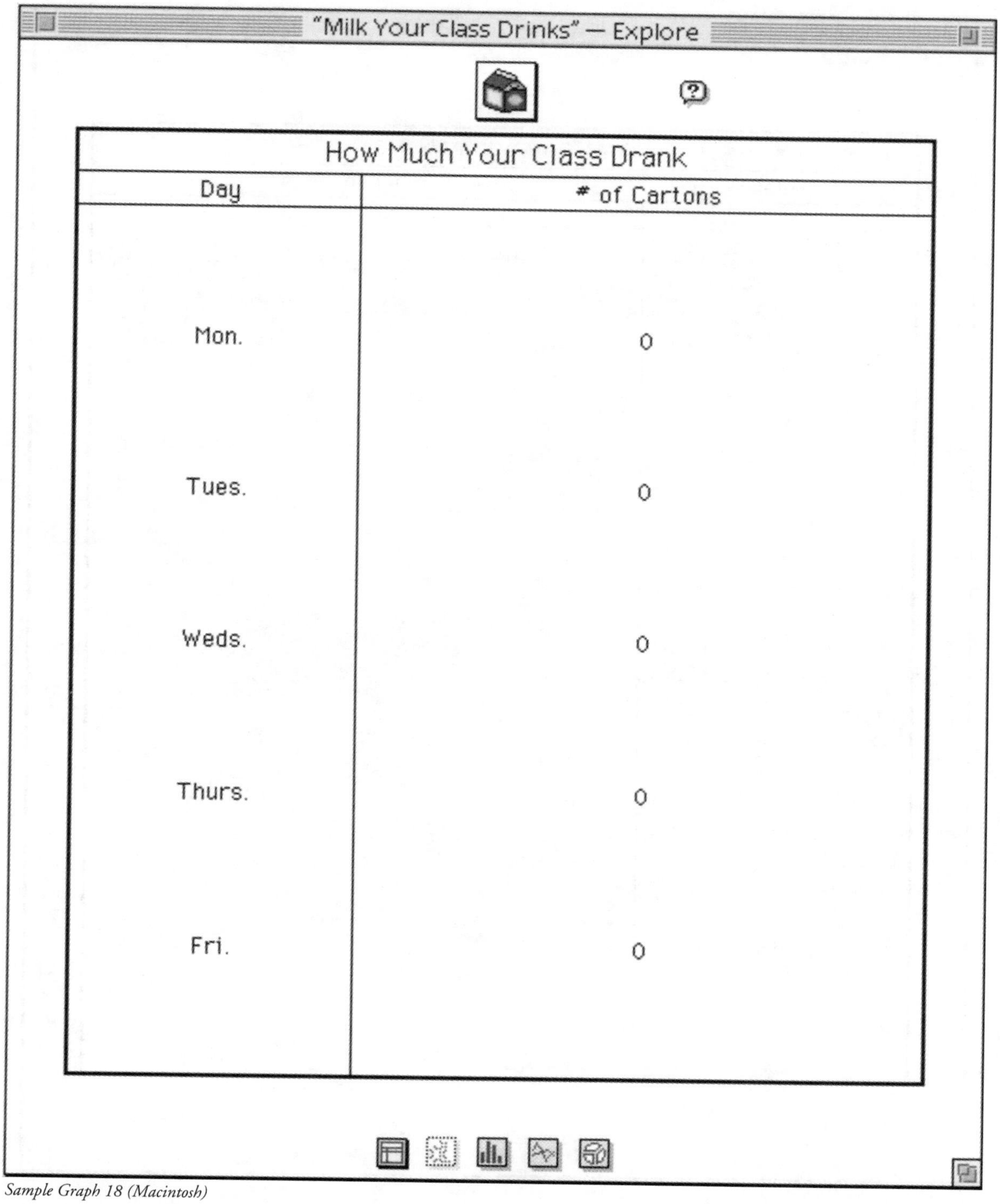

"Milk Your Class Drinks" — Explore

How Much Your Class Drank

Day	# of Cartons
Mon.	0
Tues.	0
Weds.	0
Thurs.	0
Fri.	0

Sample Graph 18 (Macintosh)

Graph 19: Sunny Days

Keep track of how many sunny days you have for five weeks and graph the data. *If you were a sunflower, during which week would you have been the happiest? Use your graph to answer the question!*

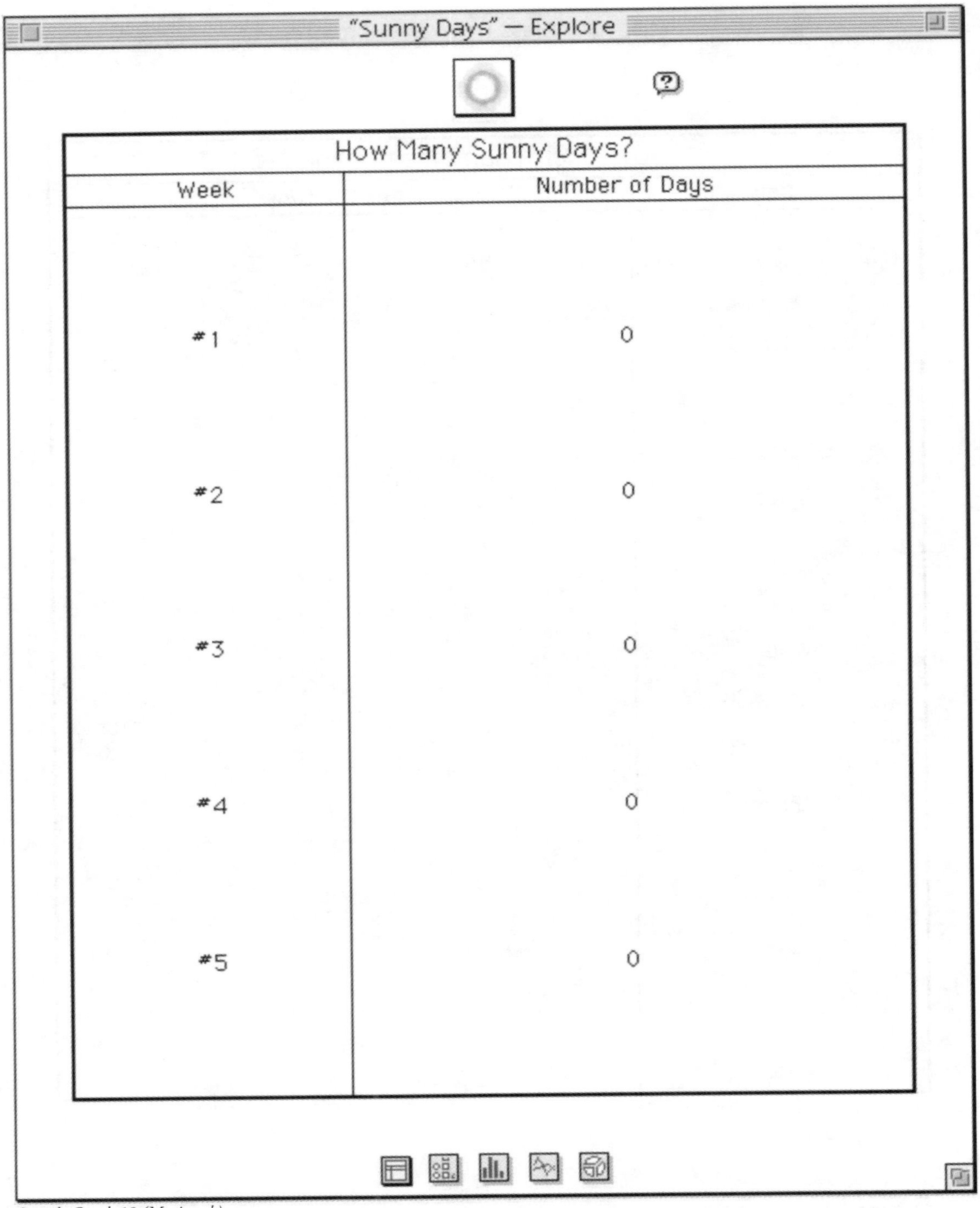

	"Sunny Days" — Explore	
	○ ⑦	

How Many Sunny Days?

Week	Number of Days
#1	0
#2	0
#3	0
#4	0
#5	0

Sample Graph 19 (Macintosh)

Graph 20: Teeth You've Lost

Have students work in teams of five and graph how many teeth they've lost.
(Print each graph.) *If the Tooth Fairy gave out a gold coin for every lost tooth,
who would have the most gold coins?* Use your graphs to answer the question!

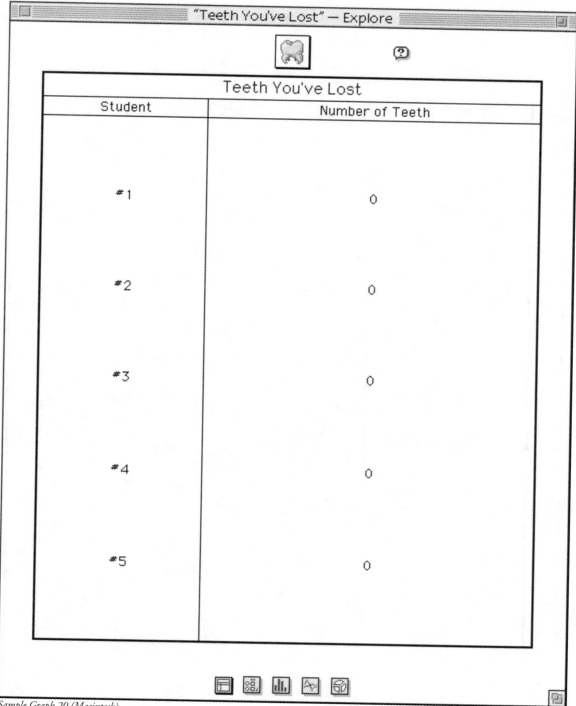

Sample Graph 20 (Macintosh)

Graph 21: Weather Forecast

Make predictions for what you think the weather will be like exactly one week from today. Graph your data, then print and post your graph, and check back a week later. *How many students should think about becoming professional guessers when they grow up?* Use your graphs to answer the question!

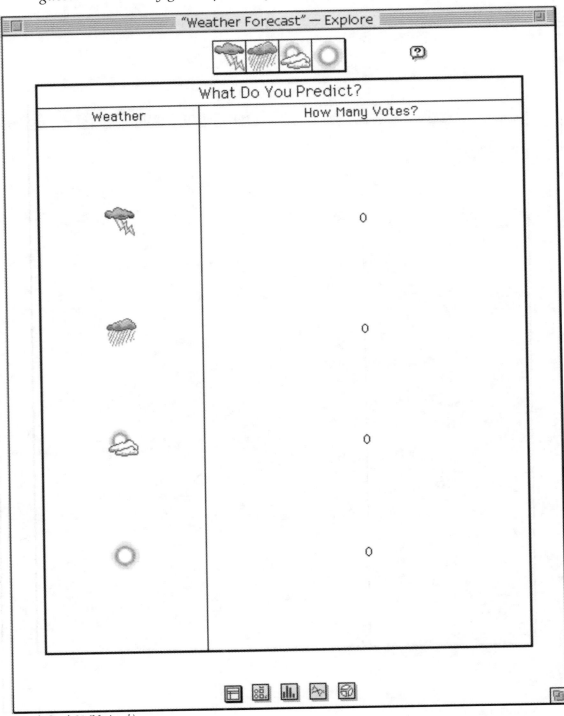

Sample Graph 21 (Macintosh)

Graph 22: What Pets Do You Have?

Make a graph of the pets you have. *If the grocery store ran out of turtle chow, how many kids would have hungry pets?* Use your graphs to answer the question!

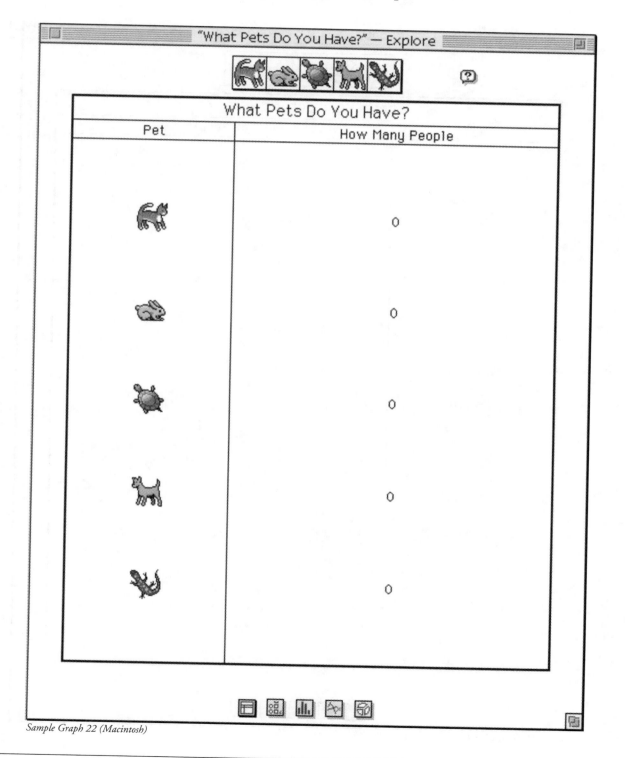

Sample Graph 22 (Macintosh)

Graph 23: What's Your Job?

Graph the jobs you do at home. *If the grass in your town grew
a foot overnight, how many kids would have a LOT of work to do?*
Use your graphs to answer the question!

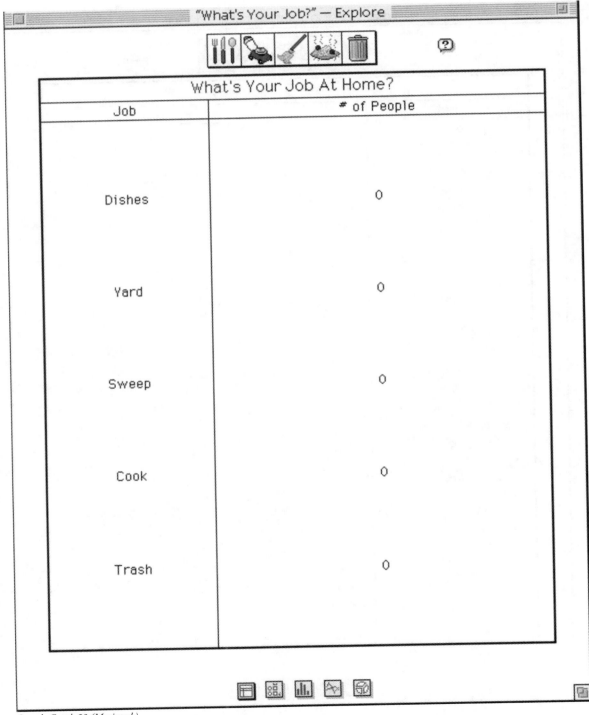

Sample Graph 23 (Macintosh)

Graph 24: You Want to Ride a WHAT???

Imagine that a very special animal circus came to town and offered rides
on different animals. Which animal would you like to ride the most?
*If the fish came down with Fish Flu and had to rest, how many students
would be disappointed?* Use your graphs to answer the question!

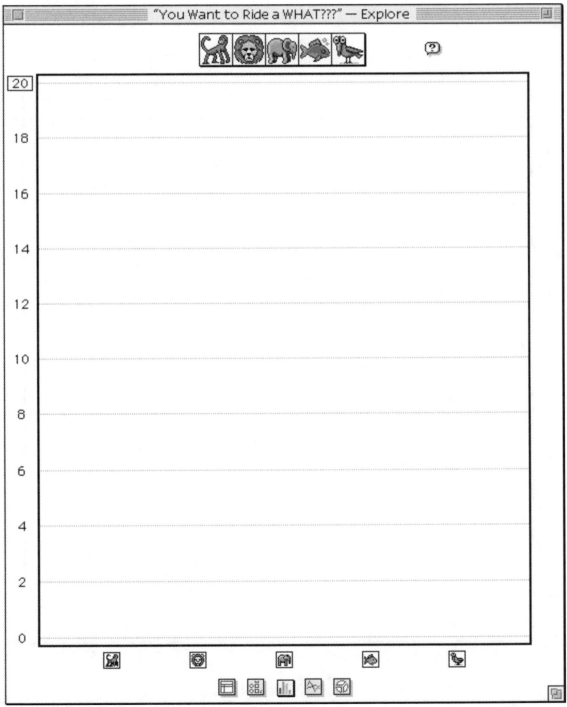

Sample Graph 24 (Macintosh)

Graph 25: Your Class Plant Has Grown!

Start a plant from seed, measure its growth over a period of weeks,
and graph the data. *Did your plant have a growth spurt or did it grow
at a slow and steady pace?* Use your graphs to answer the question!

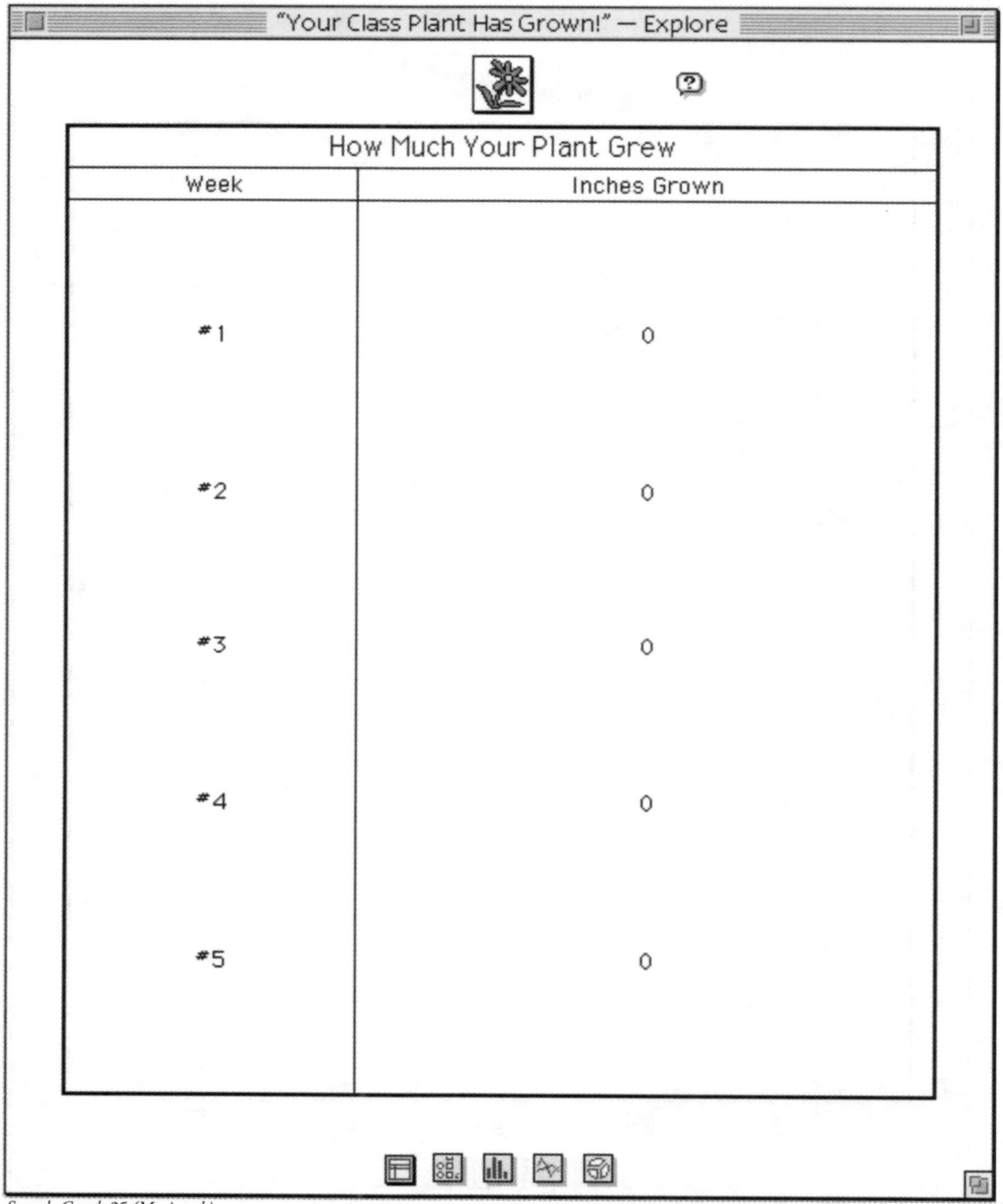

"Your Class Plant Has Grown!" — Explore

How Much Your Plant Grew

Week	Inches Grown
#1	0
#2	0
#3	0
#4	0
#5	0

Sample Graph 25 (Macintosh)

Graph 26: Match It - Birthdays!

Working as a class, in teams, or individually, create a graph that represents the data in this graph. When you've finished, click **Check My Match!** to see how well you've done!

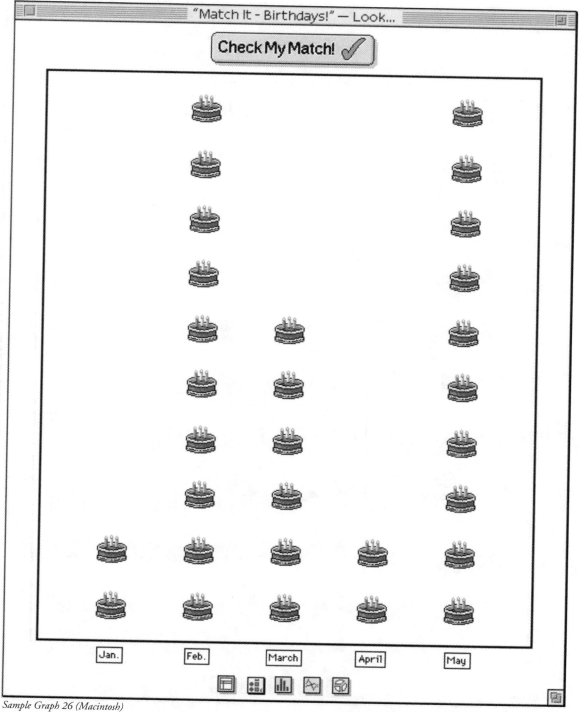

Sample Graph 26 (Macintosh)

Graph 27: Match It - Farm Animals

Working as a class, in teams, or individually, create a graph
that represents the data in this graph. When you've finished,
click **Check My Match!** to see how well you've done!

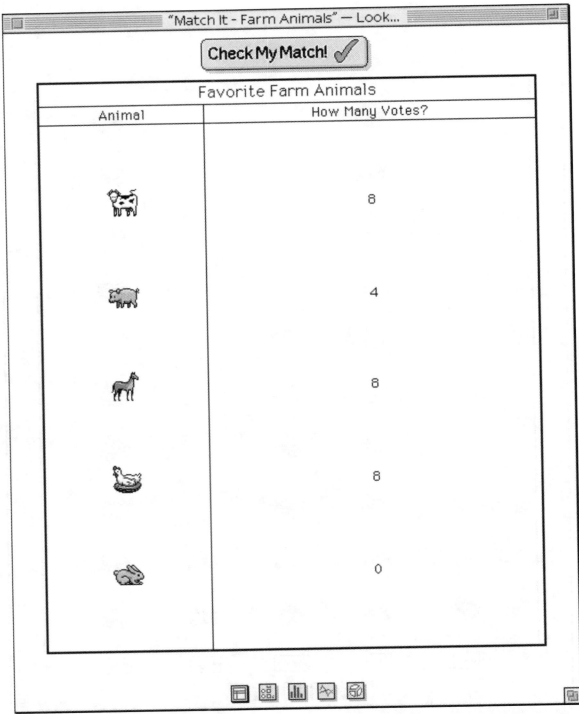

Sample Graph 27 (Macintosh)

Graph 28: Match It - Fruits

Working as a class, in teams, or individually, create a graph
that represents the data in this graph. When you've finished,
click **Check My Match!** to see how well you've done!

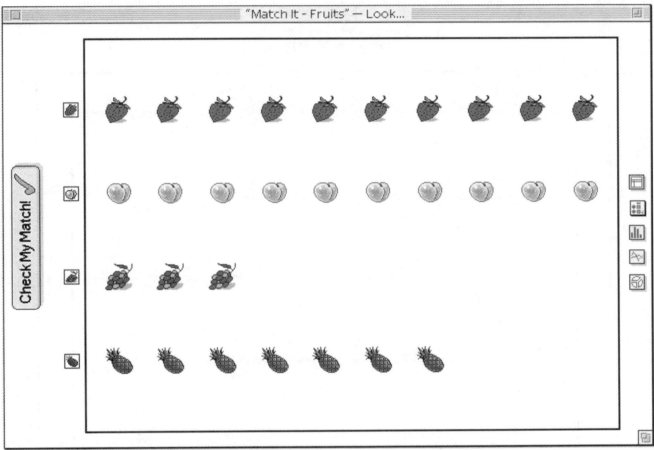

Sample Graph 28 (Macintosh)

Graph 29: Match It - Lost Teeth

Working as a class, in teams, or individually, create a graph
that represents the data in this graph. When you've finished,
click **Check My Match!** to see how well you've done!

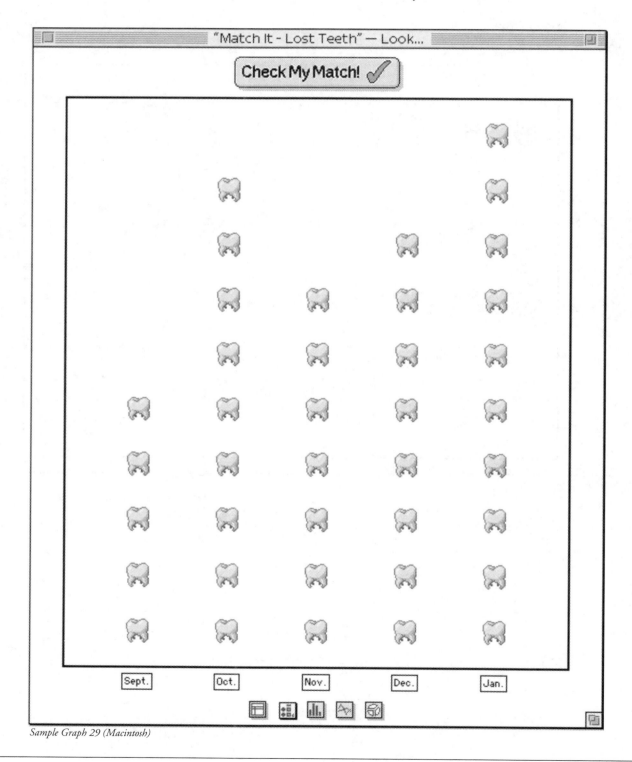

Sample Graph 29 (Macintosh)

Graph 30: Match It - Moods

Working as a class, in teams, or individually, create a graph
that represents the data in this graph. When you've finished,
click **Check My Match!** to see how well you've done!

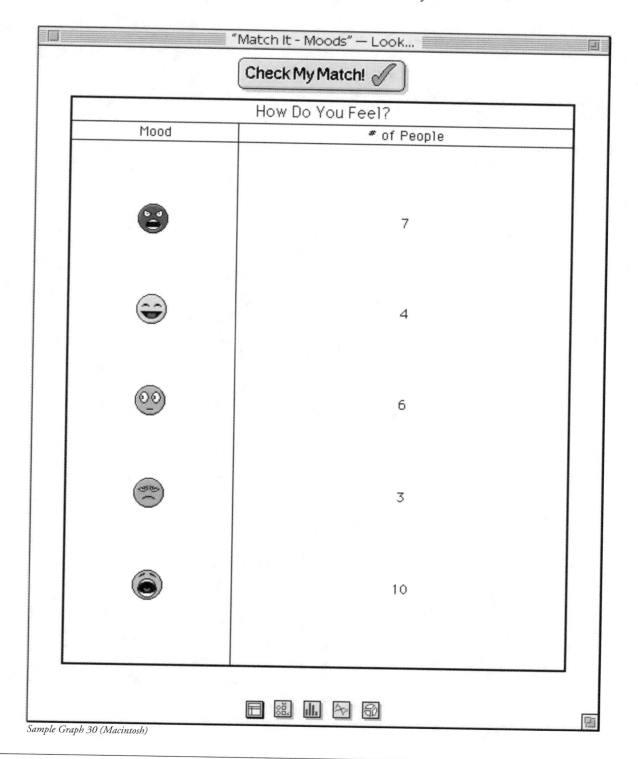

Sample Graph 30 (Macintosh)

Graph 31: Match It - More Animals

Working as a class, in teams, or individually, create a graph
that represents the data in this graph. When you've finished,
click **Check My Match!** to see how well you've done!

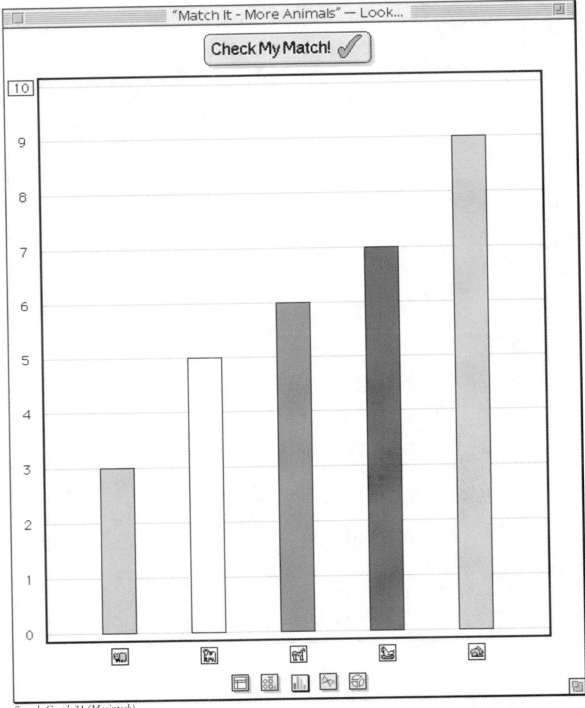

Sample Graph 31 (Macintosh)

Graph 32: Match It - Safari Animals

Working as a class, in teams, or individually, create a graph
that represents the data in this graph. When you've finished,
click **Check My Match!** to see how well you've done!

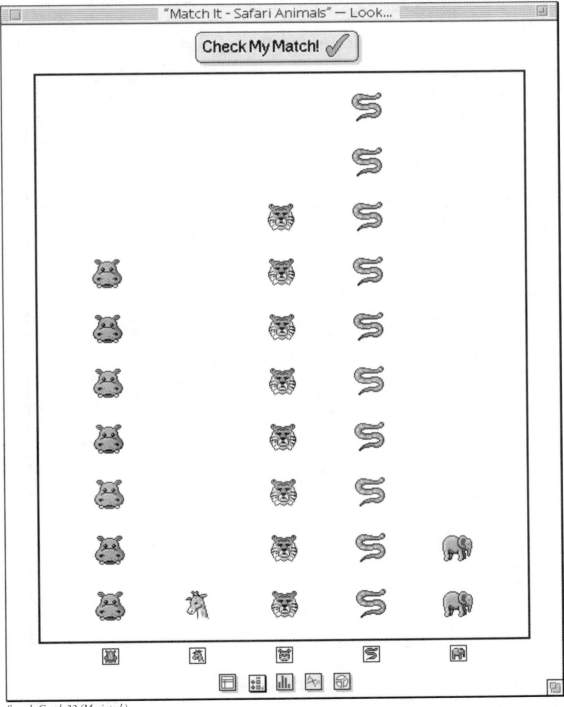

Sample Graph 32 (Macintosh)

Graph 33: Match It - Seasons

Working as a class, in teams, or individually, create a graph that represents the data in this graph. When you've finished, click **Check My Match!** to see how well you've done!

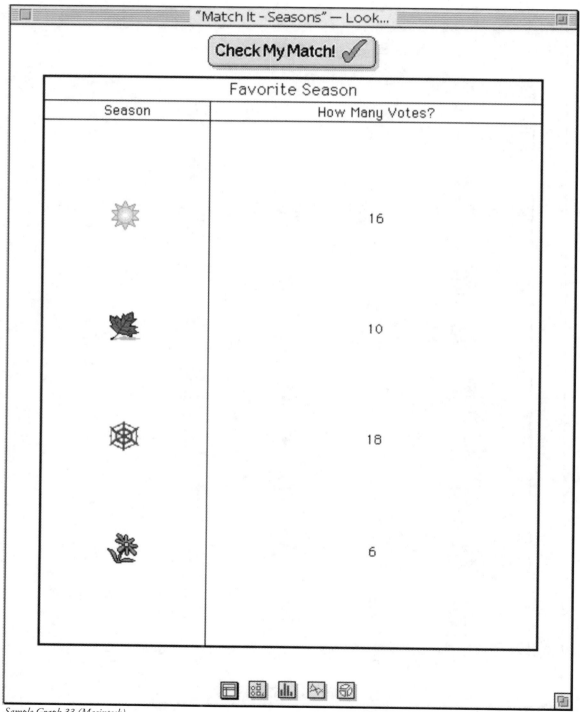

Sample Graph 33 (Macintosh)

Graph 34: Match It - Starry Night

Working as a class, in teams, or individually, create a graph
that represents the data in this graph. When you've finished,
click **Check My Match!** to see how well you've done!

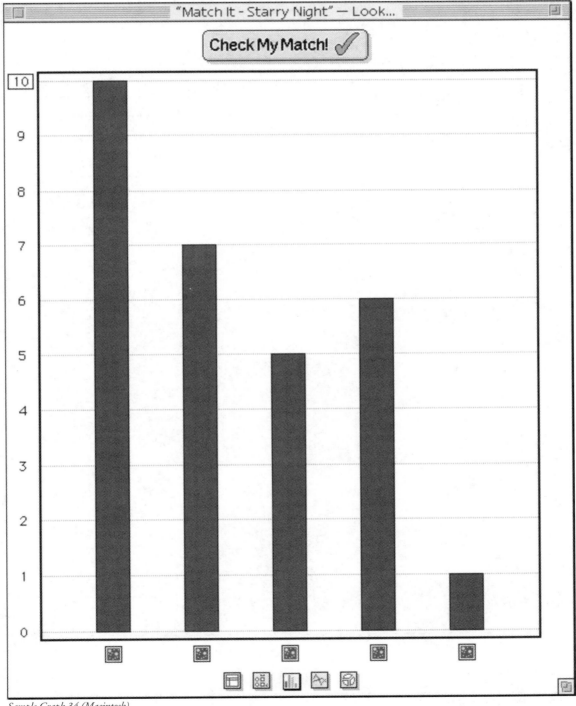

Sample Graph 34 (Macintosh)

Graph 35: Match It - Travel

Working as a class, in teams, or individually, create a graph
that represents the data in this graph. When you've finished,
click **Check My Match!** to see how well you've done!

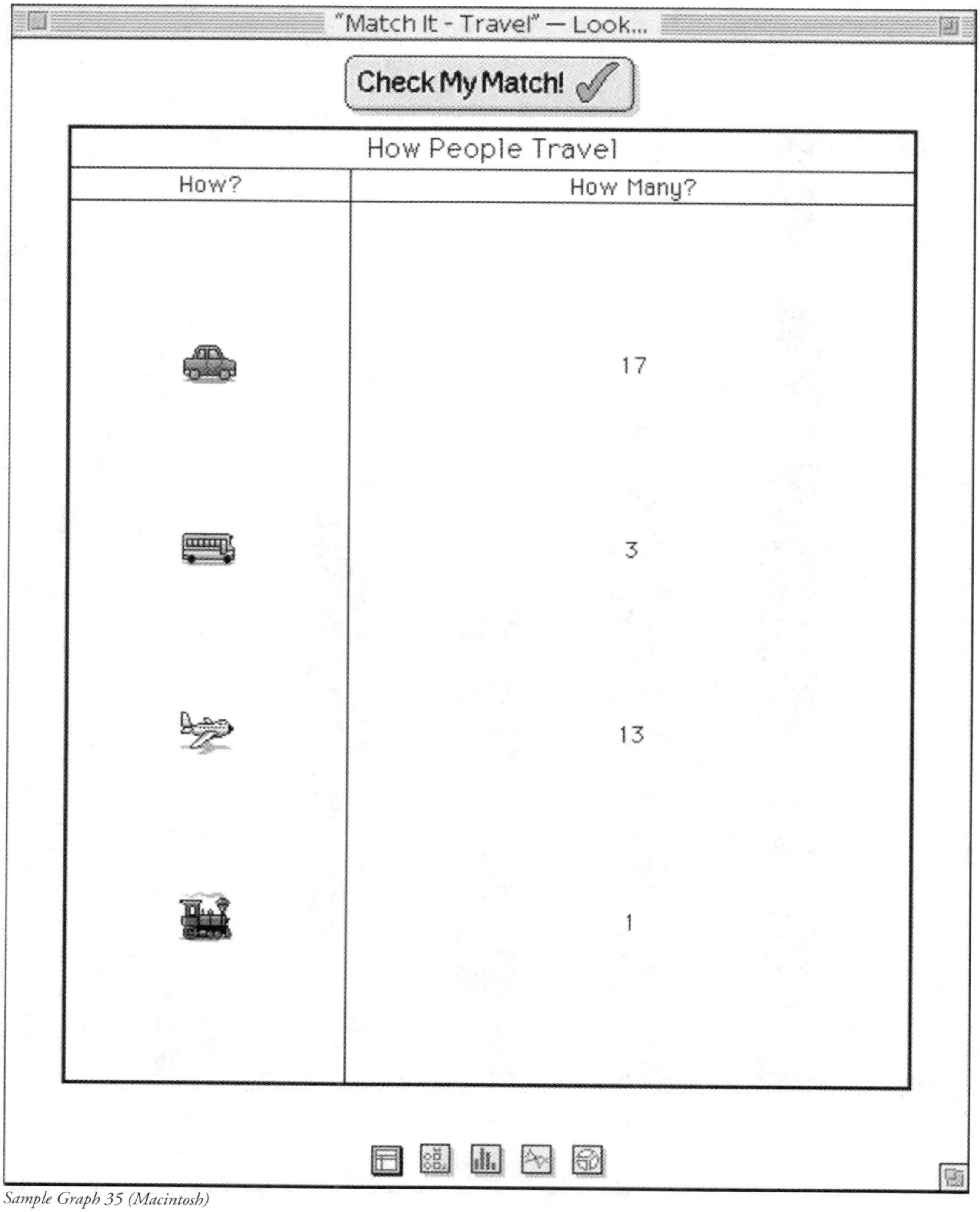

Sample Graph 35 (Macintosh)

Choosing the Right Graph

Children need to understand that different types of graphs are used to describe different kinds of data. Consider these guidelines when planning and implementing graphing activities with your class.

Table	All kinds of data
Picture	Things that can be counted
Bar	Things that can be counted or measured
Line	Things that change over time, trends
Circle	Parts of a whole, parts of a set

The following practices can encourage students to develop skills in identifying appropriate ways of displaying different types of data:

- Display different representations of the same data side by side for comparison.

- Use the Graph Type buttons to change data instantly from one representation to another.

- Ask students which type of graph is easiest for them to understand. Which graph do they think makes the most sense? Ask students to give reasons for their opinions.

- Encourage students to examine the ways data is displayed in newspapers, magazines, television, textbooks, and other media.

- Guide students in making generalizations about the types of data best displayed by each graph type.

Getting Started in the Primary Grades

The following suggestions can help assure success when introducing graphing concepts and activities in the primary grades.

Start with counting, classifying, and sorting activities.
Have students count objects, determine categories, and sort. Then have them come up with new categories and sort again.

Use manipulatives. Provide extensive experience with concrete activities before moving on to abstract concepts. (See Working with Manipulatives on pages 76–78.)

Encourage students to devise their own systems.
Ask students how they would display data and have them design imaginative displays using manipulatives, diagrams, and graphs.

Start by graphing real objects. Create people graphs, object graphs, and block graphs.

Move on to representational graphs. Use pictures, drawings, and photographs of real objects. These semi-concrete representations help students make a transition to more abstract forms of graphing.

Make the transition to abstract representations. Introduce the use of uniform ideographs or symbols in the form of picture graphs. Then move on to bar, line, and circle graphs.

Limit the number of graph elements. Start with graphs that include only two groups or graph elements. Gradually increase the number of groups.

Select topics to which children can relate. Young children are curious about themselves and the world around them. Take advantage of this natural curiosity by selecting topics of interest to your students. Encourage students to suggest graphing activities and enlist their help in identifying appropriate categories for sorting and classifying data.

Provide a meaningful context. Graphing will make more sense and students will internalize concepts better if graphing activities are presented in meaningful contexts.

Build graphing activities around a theme. When planning additional graphing activities, try to organize them around an ongoing project or theme. Activities that are drawn from everyday classroom experiences will have the advantage of a meaningful context.

Print. A printed copy makes the abstract more concrete and allows students to share their work.

Talk math, write math. Learning and using the language of math and graphing will help students internalize concepts. The ability to type a story or description when printing graphs encourages students to "write math." You may want to culminate graphing activities with creative writing and drawing activities.

Encourage confidence. Success builds confidence. Taking students through a progression of easy to more difficult graphing activities will encourage success and build confidence as they gradually develop more sophisticated graphing skills.

Working with Manipulatives

Children's first graphing experiences should involve the use of concrete objects. From real graphs (graphs that use real objects), students should move to representational graphs (drawings, photos, pictures cut from magazines), and only then to symbolic graphs.

Use some of the following ideas for implementing concrete graphing activities, or devise your own. Try to pick topics that are conducive to the use of manipulatives. Also be sure that you encourage your students to suggest and devise original systems for displaying data.

People graphs

- Line up desks or chairs in several rows to create a grid-like pattern. Assign labels to each row — e.g., blue eyes, brown eyes, black eyes, green eyes — and have students choose seats accordingly.

- Create a large reusable floor grid using heavy paper, canvas, or other fabric. Label rows and columns and have students line up accordingly.

- Use masking tape to create a floor grid or, if you have large rectangular floor tiles, use tape to mark off rows. Place labels for each row and have students line up.

Block graphs

Have students stack Unifix® cubes, building blocks, Cuisenaire® rods or any standard size blocks. If you want, students can paste pictures on blocks or use different colored blocks to represent different categories.

Object graphs

Use juice cartons, cereal boxes, shoes, hats, books, toys, stuffed animals, or any other objects. Make smaller object graphs with clothespins, tokens, beads, paper clips, plastic or paper chain links, M&M's, or similar items. Use the following suggestions or a system of your own for organizing object graphs. Better yet, let your students devise a system.

- Draw a grid on the blackboard, bulletin board, or wall. Label rows or columns and stack items or attach them with tape.

- Use the floor grid described above or create a smaller version which can also be used on a desktop.

- Create a rectangular fabric panel approximately 4' x 4' or larger. Divide the panel into squares in a grid-like pattern and sew a pocket on each section. Attach removable labels to each row and let students tuck items into pockets in the appropriate row.

- Create a large rectangular frame with pigeonholes in a grid-like pattern. Assign labels to different rows or columns and have students place one item per pigeonhole in appropriate rows.

- For small objects, make copies of the 1" graph paper on page 89. Have students sort objects, label columns, and place objects on the sheet with one per box or "cell."

- Use egg cartons as ready-made grids.

- Attach magnets in rows or columns to any magnetic surface.

- Hook together links and hang chains side by side.

- Clip clothes pins in rows to the sides or bottom of a chart.

Pictures and photographs of real objects

Have students draw pictures, cut pictures from magazines, or use photographs. Students can use photos or drawings of themselves to cast votes. Have students tape the pictures in rows or columns on the blackboard, bulletin board, or wall. If you want, place a large sheet of paper with a grid on the floor or table and label rows or columns.

Other concrete graphing activities

There are a million uses for graphs. Here are a few activity ideas that may spark some great interest:

- Have students outline their hands, feet, or entire body and then cut out their outlines and post them on the blackboard, bulletin board, or wall. Older students can draw horizontal and/or vertical axes and make appropriate labels.

- Use ribbon, cash register tape, or string to measure students' height, the circumference of their wrists, or the length or height of any object. Cut appropriate lengths and use them to create "bar graphs."

- Have students create picture graphs using rubber stamps and ink pads. Use different stamps or identical stamps with a different color ink for each column or row.

- Use string, yarn, or ribbon to connect the tops of the columns in a bar or picture graph in order to introduce students to line graphs.

- Use geoboards to create bar or line graphs.

- Use your imagination! Look around you and invent your own unique measuring units.

Printing Ideas

With *The Graph Club* you can print graphs and a whole bunch of other neat stuff including graphics from *The Graph Club Curriculum Kit* (sold separately — see page 9 for details). All graphs and graphics can be printed in three sizes: standard, big book (2 pages by 2 pages), and poster (3 pages by 3 pages). A special print dialog box encourages students to write about their graphs by providing an opportunity to enter text. This text can be saved and printed with your graphs. Here are some suggestions for making the most of *The Graph Club*'s printing features.

- Have students suggest a description or story to go with the graph and enter it in the print dialog box before printing.

- Print graphs standard size and make copies for each student in the class. Have students color their graphs and, if the text box is blank, write a description or story.

- Have students create a book composed entirely of graphs that tell a story. Print the graphs book-size, bind them together, and have students color them and write descriptions in the text boxes.

- Print graphs poster-size and have students work together to color them and write a description or story. Post the finished product in the classroom, hallway, library, or another location in the school or community.

- Insert a heat transfer ribbon in your dot matrix printer and print *The Graph Club* logo (reverse version) on regular paper to create an iron-on transfer for t-shirts or banners. Or print *The Graph Club* logo (normal version) using a regular ribbon or toner to create posters, book covers and report covers.

Authentic Assessment

The Graph Club is an effective tool for assessing student performance. It provides a means to engage students in meaningful real-world tasks and allows them to create products that can be added to their portfolios.

Have students use *The Graph Club* to complete real-world tasks such as those listed below.

+ Surveys – Ask students to pose a meaningful question, design a survey form, and collect data. Have them organize the results in graph form, interpret their findings, and tell why their findings are meaningful.

+ Field studies – Have students investigate the world around them. Ask students to count or measure plants, objects, animals or themselves, create a graph, and interpret their findings. Ask them to hypothesize to a broader sample.

+ Library research – Have students collect information from books, magazines, and other resources, organize their data, and present it in graph form. Have them summarize and interpret their findings for the class.

+ Predicting – Ask students to predict what will happen to one graph when another graph in the same data set is changed — e.g., what will happen to a circle graph when a bar graph is changed. Ask students to use their research or survey results to predict the outcome of a future endeavor.

+ Match – Use the Match mode to evaluate students' understanding of the relationship between different representations of the same data.

+ Brainstorm – Have students brainstorm as many interpretations as possible for a randomly generated graph in the Guess modes.

+ Add printed graphs and written work to students' portfolios.

Reproducible Masters

Circle Graph

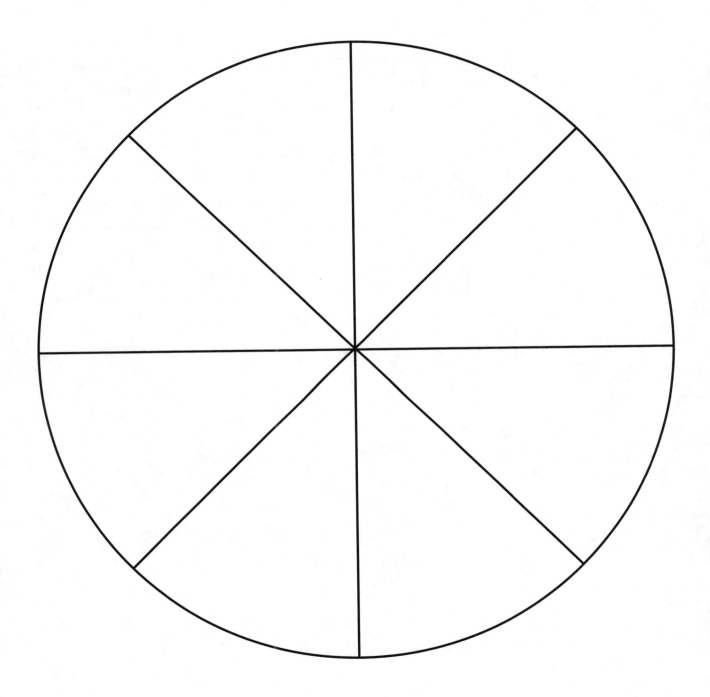

Dogs Cats Bunnies Fish

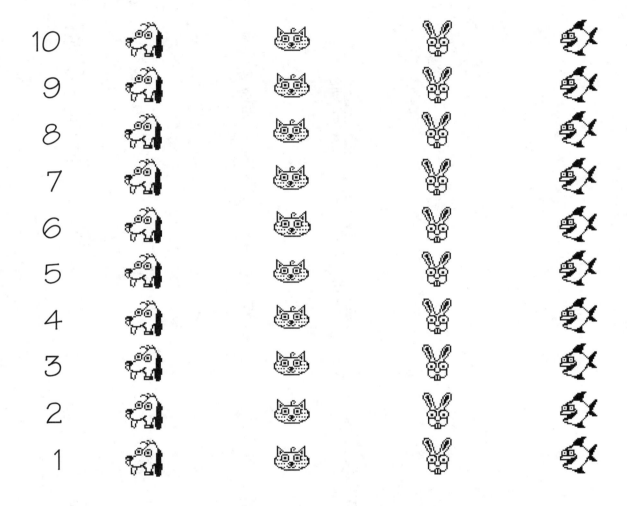

Bus Car Bicycle Foot

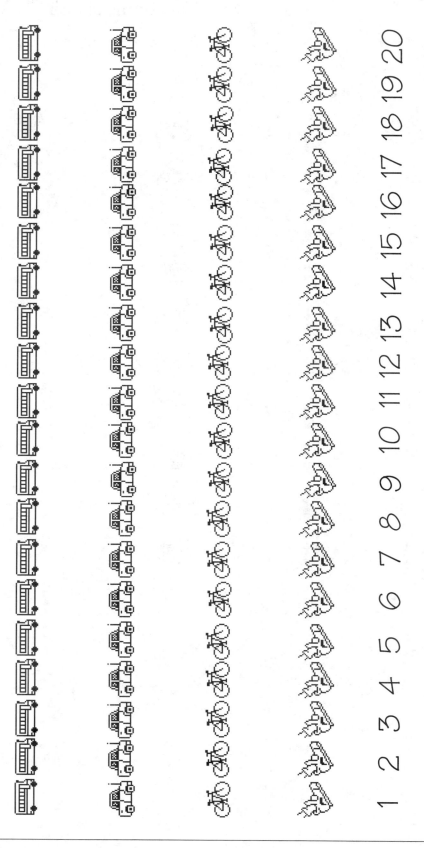

Dollar Bills

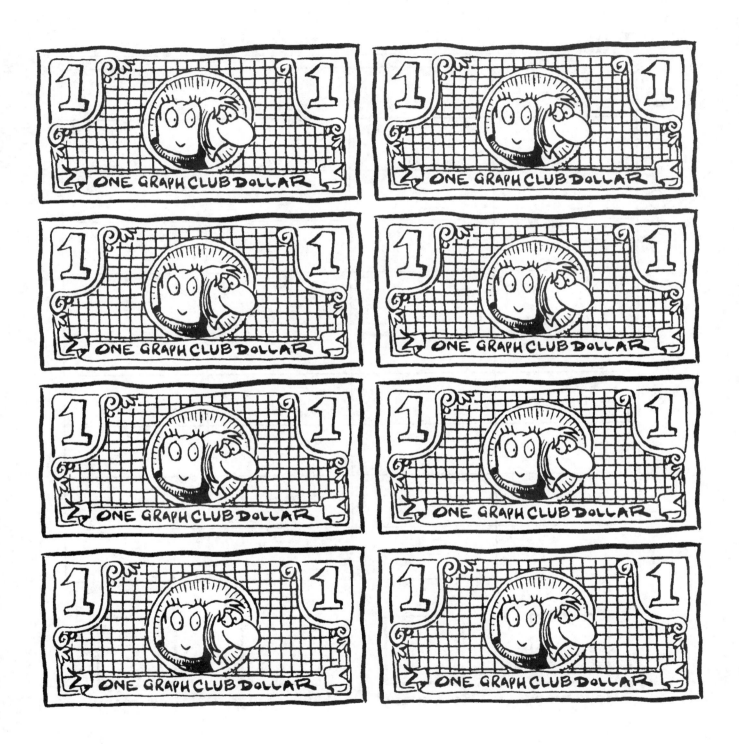

Grid

Title: _____

10			
9			
8			
7			
6			
5			
4			
3			
2			
1			

How many? **How many?** **How many?** **How many?**

1 cm x 1 cm Grid

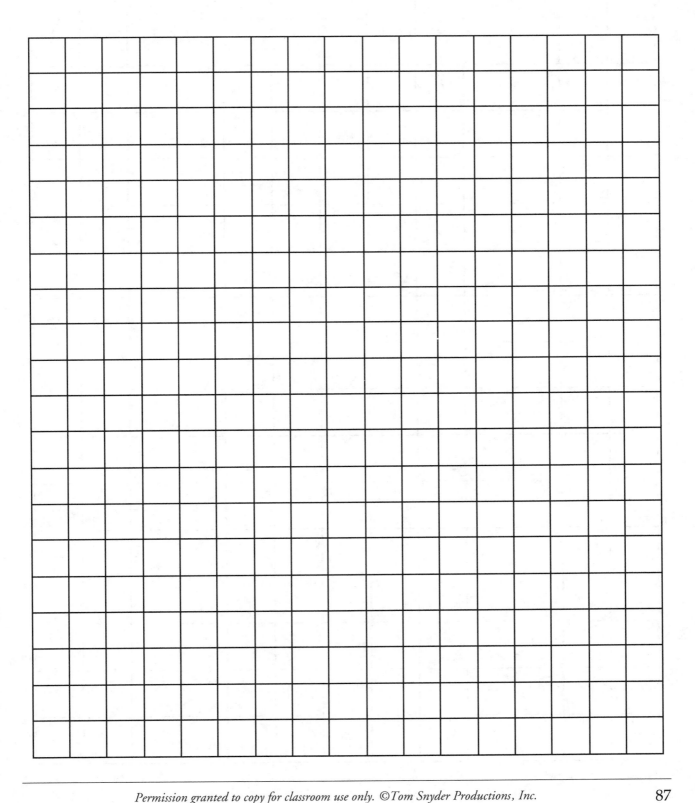

1/2 in. x 1/2 in. Grid

1 in. x 1 in. Grid

The Graph Club Logo

The Graph Club Reversible Logo

- Insert a heat transfer ribbon in your dot matrix printer and print *The Graph Club* logo (reverse version in the Print Special Menu) on regular paper to create an iron-on transfer for t-shirts or banners. Or print *The Graph Club* logo (normal version) using a regular ribbon or toner to create posters, book covers, and report covers.

Membership Cards

Additional team activities can help promote cohesiveness. Creating team paraphernalia — flags, buttons, posters — are good spirit boosters. Use this template to create team cards which can be displayed when a team, or teams, achieve a certain goal or behavior. Keep in mind that many activities designed for teams can become whole class (whole team) activities. Consider activities which incorporate all teams the way the Olympic flag includes a color from each participating nation's flag. Cooperative teamwork does not need to exclude whole class work and class spirit.

Official *Graph Club* Team Card

Team Name _____

Team Members

_____

_____

_____

_____

_____

Draw your team flag or symbol

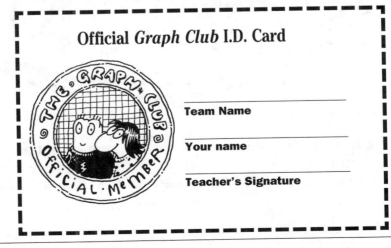

Official *Graph Club* I.D. Card

Team Name
_____

Your name
_____

Teacher's Signature

Software Icons

Ancestors

Buildings

Farm Animals

Wild Animals

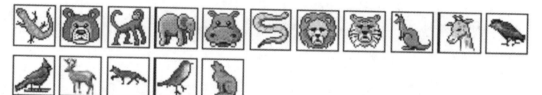

Creatures

Fruits & Vegetables

Meats & Proteins

Software Icons (cont.)

Grains & Cereal

Dairy Products

Misc. Foods

Holidays

Weather

Seasons

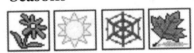

Sports

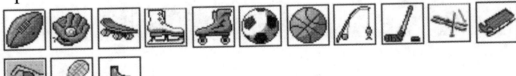

Shoes

People & Characters

Software Icons (cont.)

Trees

Transportation

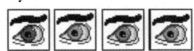

Places

Everyday Objects

Eye Color

Miscellaneous

Graphs

Money

Music

Software Icons (cont.)

Faces

Shapes

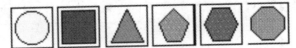

Letters and Numbers

Reading List: Counting

Each of the entries below is a counting book which lends itself to numerous graphing opportunities.

Aylesworth, Jim. *One Crow: A Counting Rhyme.* New York: Lippincott, 1988.

Baker, Jeanne. *One Hungry Spider.* London: Andre Deutsch, 1982.

Baker, Jeanne. *Window.* New York: Greenwillow, 1991.

Blumenthal, Nancy. *Count-a-saurus.* New York: Macmillan, 1989.

Bucknall, Caroline. *One Bear All Alone.* New York: Dial, 1989.

Carle, Eric. *What's For Lunch?* New York: Putnam Publishing Group, 1982.

Crews, Donald. *The Bicycle Race.* New York: Greenwillow, 1985.

Dunrea, Olivier. *Deep Down Underground.* New York: Macmillan, 1989.

Ehlert, Lois. *Fish Eyes: A Book You Can Count On.* San Diego: Harcourt Brace Jovanovich, 1990.

Froman, Robert. *Bigger and Smaller.* New York: Crowell, 1971.

Galdone, Paul. *The Little Red Hen.* New York: Seabury, 1973.

Ginsburg, Mirra. *Across the Stream.* New York: Greenwillow, 1982.

Hagne, Kathleen. *Numbears: A Counting Book.* New York: Holt, 1986.

Hammond, Franklin. *Ten Little Ducks.* New York: Scholastic, 1987.

Hoban, Russell. *Ten What?* New York: Scribners, 1974.

Hoban, Tana. *Big Ones Little Ones.* New York: Greenwillow, 1976.

Koch, Michelle. *Just One More.* New York: Greenwillow, 1989.

Leedy, Loreen. *A Number of Dragons.* New York: Holiday House, 1985.

Medearis, Angela. *Picking Peas for a Penny.* Austin, TX: State House, 1990.

Noll, Sally. *Off and Counting.* New York: Greenwillow, 1984.

O'Neill, Mary. *Take a Number.* Garden City, NY: Doubleday, 1968.

Peek, Merle. *The Balancing Act: A Counting Song.* New York: Clarion, 1987.

Pomerantz, Charlotte. *The Mango Tooth.* New York: Greenwillow, 1977.

Rockwell, Anne F. *Willy Can Count.* New York: Arcade Publishing, 1989.

Russo, Marisabina. *Only Six More Days.* New York: Greenwillow, 1988.

Sendak, Maurice. *Seven Little Monsters.* New York: Harper and Row, 1977.

Sherrow, Victoria. *Wilbur Waits.* New York: Harper and Row, 1990.

Shulevitz, Uri. *One Monday Morning.* New York: Scribner, 1967.

Tafuri, Nancy. *Who's Counting?* New York: Greenwillow, 1986.

Tudor, Tasha. *1 is One.* New York: H. Z. Walck, 1956.

Walsh, Ellen S. *Mouse Count.* San Diego: Harcourt Brace Jovanovich, 1991.

Wood, Audrey. *The Napping House.* San Diego: Harcourt Brace Jovanovich, 1984.

Reading List: Math & Language Arts

The following books will spark many graphing ideas and provide an excellent way to combine math and language arts.

Anno and Nazaki. *Anno's Mysterious Multiplying Jar.* New York: Philomel Books, 1983. Groups, bundles and bunches are highlighted in this beautifully illustrated book of multiplication.

Anno, Mitsumasa. *Anno's Counting Book.* New York: Harper Junior Books, 1977. This wordless counting book provides many opportunities for sorting and categorizing common objects.

Archambault, John. *Counting Sheep.* New York: Trumpet Club, 1989. *Counting Sheep* provides a most animal silly tale that reinforces counting, graphing, sorting and classification.

Bang, Molly. *Ten, Nine, Eight.* New York: Greenwillow, 1983. The nighttime routine is fulfilled as a father and a young child prepare for bed. Counting backwards from ten, they explore sets of objects in the quiet room.

Butler, Christina. *Too Many Eggs — A Counting Book.* Boston: D. R. Godine, 1988. What happens when Mrs. Beau forgets how many eggs she has placed in the birthday cake mix? This counting book addresses whole numbers to 20.

Carle, Eric. *My Very First Book of Numbers.* New York: Trumpet Club, 1974. This counting book provides realistic illustrations for the numbers 1 through 10.

Carle, Eric. *1, 2, 3 To The Zoo.* New York: World, 1968. This counting book takes the reader on a field trip to the zoo where the animals teach the concept of numbers.

Crews, Donald. *Ten Black Dots.* New York: Greenwillow, 1986. This book reinforces numbers 1 – 10. Presented in poetic genre, *Ten Black Dots* features two different pictures for each number.

Dee, Ruby. *Two Ways to Count to Ten.* New York: Henry Holt, 1988. This counting book reinforces the sequence of numbers to 10.

Feelings, Muriel. *Moja Means One (Swaahili Counting Book).* New York: Pied Piper Books, 1971. Number words 1 to 10 are reinforced in this unique book. Scenes depicting the natural landscape and village life are used to illustrate each Swaahili number word from one to ten.

Giganti, P. *How Many Snails?* New York: Greenwillow, 1988. This predictable story presents a set of three classification questions for each of its illustrations, and provides an excellent interactive story for any age.

Gray, Catherine. *One, Two, Three, and Four. No More?* Boston: Houghton Mifflin, 1988. This catchy story provides several opportunities for the students to count and sort.

Grossman, V. and Long, S. *Ten Little Rabbits.* San Francisco: Chronicle Books, 1991. This book not only reinforces counting, but also highlights various Native American traditions.

Hoban, Tana. *Count and See.* New York: Collier Books, 1972. A unique book in which each photograph is accompanied by three representations of a number: the large numeral, the number word, and a series of dots.

Hutchins, Pat. *1 Hunter*. New York: Greenwillow, 1982. *1 Hunter* is a unique counting book that children will surely enjoy.

Hutchins, Pat. *The Doorbell Rang*. New York: Greenwillow, 1986. Read and find out what happens as the children learn to divide their cookies evenly among each person who rings the doorbell.

Kellogg, Steven. *Much Bigger Than Martin*. New York: Dial Books, 1976. Find out the importance of size in this humorous story about Martin.

Kitamura, Satoshi. *When Sheep Cannot Sleep*. New York: Farrar, Straus & Giroux, 1986. What happens when sheep cannot sleep? Find out in this predictable book that reinforces counting concepts.

Kitchen, Bert. *Animal Numbers*. New York: Dial Books, 1987. Number concepts are highlighted in this book of animals and their offspring.

Lindbergh, Reeve. *The Midnight Farm*. New York: Dial Books, 1987. In this gentle and reassuring counting book, a sensitive mother helps her child understand how the darkness of night can provide comfort and safety.

Lionni, Leo. *Inch by Inch*. New York: Astor-Honor, 1960. A unique twist is presented in this story of a quick-thinking inchworm who saves his life by offering to measure the birds who want to eat him.

MacCarthy, Patricia. *Ocean Parade*. New York: Dial Books, 1990. Ocean life is creatively portrayed in this unique counting book.

Mack, Stan. *Ten Bears in My Bed*. New York: Pantheon, 1974. In this countdown book, ten bears have crowded into a small boy's bed and he wants them out. One by one they leave in the most delightful ways.

McMillan, Bruce. *Counting Wildflowers*. New York: Lothrop, Lee & Shepard, 1986. This book uses a series of color photographs to represent the counting numbers from 1 to 20.

Merriam, Eve. *Train Leaves the Station*. New York: Trumpet Club, 1988.

Morozumi, Atsuko. *One Gorilla*. New York: Farrar, Straus & Giroux, 1990. Number concepts are presented in this humorous counting book.

Trinca, Rod and Argent, Kerry. *One Wooly Wombat*. New York: Kane/Miller, 1982. This counting book introduces the reader to Australian animals. Number concepts are reinforced throughout this text.

Wood, Jakki. *One Bear with Bees in His Hair*. New York: Trumpet Club, 1990. This humorous story combines number concepts, rhyming words and appealing illustrations that bring the text to life.

Index

 **Tom Snyder Productions**®

80 Coolidge Hill Road • Watertown, MA 02472-5003 • USA
Phone 1-800-342-0236 • Fax 617-926-6222 • www.teachtsp.com

XGRP GRP U 09